American Bison (*Bison americanus*).

The Autobiography of a Brown Buffalo

Chapter One

I stand naked before the mirror. Every morning of my life I have seen that brown belly from every angle. It has not changed that I can remember. I was always a fat kid. I suck it in and expand an enormous chest of two large hunks of brown tit. Possibly a loss of a pound here, a pound there? I put my hands to the hips, sandbaked elbows out like wings, and turn profiled to the floor-length reflection. I tighten, suck at the air and recall that Charles Atlas was a ninety-nine-pound weakling when the beach bully kicked sand in his girl friend's pretty face. Perhaps my old mother was right. I should lay off those Snicker bars, those liverwurst sandwiches with gobs of mayonnaise and those Goddamned caramel sundaes. But look, if I suck it in just a wee bit more, push that bellybutton up against the back; can you see what will surely come to pass if you but rid yourself of this extra flesh? Just think of all the broads you'll get if you trim down to a comfortable 200.

I hold my breath too long. The blood rushes to my head and reddens my perfectly structured ears—my single bodily perfection. Grumbling and convulsions in the empty pit. I enter the bathroom and struggle to the toilet. With my large, peasant hands carefully on the rim of white, I descend to my knocked knees. I stare into the repository of all that is unacceptable and wait for the green

11

bile, my sunbaked face where my big, brown ass will soon sit.

I strain to vomit, pushing upward with my diaphragm, with as total control of the belly as any good clarinet player could have . . . but nothing comes except gurgling convulsions from down under.

"Puke, you sonofabitch!" I command. "Aren't you the world's champion pukerupper?"

I think of garbage, dirty toilets, whiskey and gravies, but nothing happens . . . a meaningless belch and noiseless fart are all I get for my troubles on this first day of July, 1967.

"Jesus Christ, not even my body obeys me anymore!"

I sit on the bowl and face myself in the mirror above the sink. An outrageously angry face stares me down and I laugh at the sight of a Brown Buffalo sitting on his throne. But who really knows? Who can say for sure what causes ulcers? At the age of twenty-one, six (6) different doctors showed me pictures of what *they claimed* were holes in my stomach. Perhaps it really is a physical thing. They *did* tell me to lay off the booze, the hot sauce and the spicy gravies.

I stare into the mirror for an answer. See that man with the insignificant eyes drawn back, lips thinned down tight? That suave motherfucker is Mister Joe Cool himself. Yes, old Bogey . . . And now with the upper lip tightly curled under and baring the top row of white teeth, can't you tell? See how he nods his head, shaking it from side to side as in a tremble of uncontrollable anger? Right! James Cagney, you rotten scabs! And if you loosen up a bit, puff those fat cheeks out slightly and talk deep in your throat with the chewed-up cigar sticking you in the face . . . my name is Edward G. Robinson and I don't want any trouble from you guys. See?

"Constipation? How in the fuck can I be constipated when I have so much to offer?" I ask all three of them quietly.

I analyze my medical condition. It's true I refused the advice of all six doctors. For Christ's sake, I was only twenty-one. What value is a life without booze and Mexican food? Can you just imagine me drinking two quarts of milk every day for the rest of my life? They said, "Nothing hot or cold, nothing spicy and absolutely nothing alcoholic." Shit, I couldn't be *bland* if my life depended on it.

I strain, I struggle and I force the issue. "But from what?" I demand an explanation. "Could it be the fifteen-cent pineapple pie? Tin poisoning in the Campbell soup? The Doctor Pepper with peanuts floating on top?"

My three favorite men in the mirror have no answer for me.

12

I doubt they take my squawking seriously. They know I can handle it.

"Maybe it's the beancake with the blackbean sauce I got from Wing Lee's last night."

And out of the corner that faint voice of Dr. Serbin, my Jewish shrink butts in. "Don't tell me you believe that stuff about Chinese putting the leftovers back in?"

"I didn't say that!" I scream at him. Lately Dr. Serbin has taken to following me wherever I go. But certainly I wouldn't blame the skinny old Chinese man with the long, pointed beard for any of my troubles. God, I got through law school only because Wing Lee served me hot rolls of pork and chicken with a pot of tea for twenty-five cents every morning at the corner of Hyde & Jackson Streets where I've lived these past five years. How could I possibly have anything but good to say of that inscrutable old gentleman, who has not spoken one single word in all that time except once to say, "No pork buns today. Chicken."

"Did anything unusual happen yesterday?" the good psychiatrist asks while I wipe my ass with perfumed paper.

"Oh, don't start on that. I'm *constipated!* Can't you see? It's a Goddamned *physical* thing!"

"But surely there's a reason," he stabs with a feigned sobriety. "You must be holding something back."

"Ah, that's bullshit!"

"What's bullshit?"

"Everything's bullshit! You and your accusations. All of them . . . they're just Jewish fairy tales."

I laugh and shake my head at him. But he fails to respond. He has no sense of humor, that skinny Jew with the tweed coat and answers to everything. Fucking tall intellectual bastard, doesn't even know how to laugh when a good line is thrown him.

Then without warning, a belch of brown water gasps out of my waves of yellow lard. I smile serenely.

"You see, nothing to it," I mock my shrink. "It's just the etcetera diet of a kid with ulcers like I've been telling you all along."

He fits a king size Kool to his ivory holder, snaps the golden lighter, leans back, crosses his legs and blows the white smoke in my direction.

"So you come here for treatment of ulcers. Is that what you're saying?"

I refuse to continue the conversation with that Ivy League, black-haired bastard. He is unfair, that Jewish shrink of mine. He takes advantage of my condition. He wouldn't dare talk that way to me on the street. If we were on my turf, you can bet your ass he wouldn't hound me the way he does in his hot-shit office with me flat on my back. But I have no appeal. There's no court of last resort when you lay plastered to his black leather couch telling him all your dirty stories which you know damned well he repeats to rouged Pacific Heights matrons over cocktails and chicken-shit crackers with dry salami from North Beach.

No sir, the shrink is the final arbiter. He gets the last laugh so long as you pay your bill, a little matter which I've overlooked for the past six months now. That's right, I've refused to pay my bill and refused to talk for a long time. I've found that my only salvation lies in silence. Perfect quiet with your index finger to your lips. Just don't say a word. Let him put his foot in his mouth. You just shut up. And no matter how much he threatens to cut you off, no matter how snotty his little business notes get, even when he personally underlines them in red ink, no matter how he sighs at the end of an hour of silence, you know that your only hope is to ignore him.

But even that doesn't work anymore. Ever since he took to following me I've found it rather difficult to ignore him. He's become a veritable monkey on my back. When I refuse to talk he digs into my kaleidoscopic brain with his chemistry set. He hovers over me, pushes me off my seat and crowds me into the corner with those fucking electrical pills of his. He interrupts conversations like a man without culture. When I interview clients, make demands upon superior court judges, when I sit and down scotches with my friends at Trader JJ's, even then that skinny fag without character butts in and spoils things for me.

Can you understand what it feels to wake up late at night with only the sounds of cable cars jerking along Hyde and foghorns down the street at Aquatic Park? There you are, staring hot-eyed at the ceiling, the beast in your anxious hand in the darkness of the night sweating it over some hot fantasy you want to stab before she gets away and suddenly you hear him breathing quietly, observing you from his chair and saying something cute like, "Who do *you* think she is?" Implying, of course that *he* knows who she is, but he just wants to give you a crack at it first. I despise men with show-off knowledge. Wisdom should be freely available to all men without smart-alecky impediments. And so I add a touch or two, make the dream more dramatic, a little more action here and there. Then I smile when he interprets the bugger for me.

I especially like it when he says, "That really wasn't Alice you strangled in the bathtub. It was her boyfriend, Ted."

Jesus H. Christ! And to think, he actually gets twenty-five bucks an hour—or rather, forty-five minutes—for that nonsense. So, what I usually do when I catch him in my room interrupting my fantasies, I simply take another of those green jobs with chloroform, rip me off a piece, lay back and wait for the clock hand to turn.

But now with my bowels relieved I arise from my *sitio* and enter my favorite room—the shower. Every morning of my life I cleanse myself. I am never out of soap. In whatever home I may happen to be, in any weather, I always take a shower. I turn on the hot without the cold and watch the steam make bubbles on my long brown arms. Because I am a smooth man without hair the steam burns me more than normal people. But I grit my teeth and part my lips like old Bogart, the only man who has never failed me. I clench my fists and tighten my body as the steam burns into my chest.

"Shit, I can take anything," I say for my hero's approval. "They'll never make *me* talk!"

He cocks the brim of his gangster hat and says, "Sure, kid Just hang tough."

And when the sneaky Japs in khaki uniforms and beanie caps see that I'll die before I talk, they turn off the hot steam suddenly and immediately turn on the freezing cold water.

"Christ, are they serious?" I show no change in emotion. I absolutely do not flinch. They'll get nothing out of me. I look straight ahead. My entire body, my face and my thoughts remain static. Even Tojo would appreciate this. Whatever torture man might devise is of no consequence to me. I am resigned, stoical—the existential man.

Bogey pats me on the back. "Okay, kid. You did a good job. Now finish her off."

Quickly I equalize the hot with the cold and hurry to indulge myself before she gets away. With warm water and pure Palmolive-green suds for a teaser the little bugger enlarges, swells and expands before my very eyes. And miracle of miracles, it grows while I peek through the keyhole.

Just look at that! She is taking off her dress. She can't quite reach the zipper down her back. There is no one in this house but me. I know that soon she'll call for someone to assist . . . I do nothing but bulge my eyes and wait. I don't even have to touch it. See how I twist the spray to a single, hard stream that strikes against the brown protrusion? Isn't that a clearly innocent act? Am I to blame? Did I tell her to leave that little hole open? Did

I intentionally conjure up that image? What have I to do with her predicament? If she had longer arms, if they had made those white uniforms with the zipper in front, if she had hung a towel over the door knob none of this would have happened. But instead she bends over to take off those phony nylon stockings they use now since Tojo stopped sending Japanese silk.

The kid rips into the bathroom. "Did you call?"

"I called for your dad, *malcriado!*" she says with anger.

"But he's in Okinawa," the kid pleads with unmistakable logic.

"That's right. I forgot."

"The letter said he didn't know *when* the war would be over. And the paper said Tojo is still alive."

The woman sighs, nods her head. Perhaps a tear comes down.

"Okay. You can help me with my zipper."

With her back to him he unhooks the snap and slowly pulls it down to her waist.

And quickly, before the water loses its warmth I call upon Alice, my friend's old lady with the short, blonde hair and silver lips. Would she mind being unfaithful just this one time?

"But Oscar, what would Ted say?" She has a high, nasal voice without conviction. I know she is just dying to get into the shower with me. I can tell by the way she always asks me if I'm hungry when I visit them before I go to see my shrink. A hundred times (while the fat seaman from Brooklyn with the Irish accent plays with himself), a million times I've seen the long, fine legs of this Swedish babe from Minnesota just wiggle up and down the kitchen, her shaking that beautiful ass in front of me to get me out of my depression. That's what she says. But I know that secretly, down deep inside she wants me to grab her graceful neck, twist those soft, long arms of hers and jam her into the shower so I can nibble away at those delectable, dainty breasts of warm, white meat that I suck now as the brown giant explodes.

The fucking shrink steps into the shower and says, "Did you ever stop to consider that it might simply be a form of self-love?" He'll probably bill me for cleaning his tweed coat, he's so determined to get at me.

"Christ, you make better excuses than I do." I shove him out of my way and begin to prepare for my clients. I finish my toiletry, I dab on a bit of Old Spice, spray some Right Guard up my crotch just in case I happen to run into some woman, and I punctually take my pills for the day's work. Then I rush headlong into the traffic in my trusty green Plymouth that my father got for me when I passed the Bar a year ago this month.

16

Chapter Two

 I leave my Polk District apartment and drive through the tunnel under Russian Hill on Broadway, where the sidewalks are covered with ants in Brooks Bros. clothing, computers with simple black brief cases, fancy umbrellas in hand, wearing good old slick loafers to get you down to Montgomery Street, the richest street on the West Coast. I cast a glance or two at the giant pictures of zoftig girls with silicone boobs, Carol Doda and The Persian Lamb who chained herself to the Golden Gate Bridge rather than leave her husband—all coming at me from the fronts of tourist traps, Topless Joints with fat Filipino barkers dragging in the customers out for a score or at least a hard-on.

The girls are in leather pants, black boots and long hair. Christ, what happened to the culture of the fifties? Don't these silly females from Toledo know this is San Francisco? They always used to wear gloves and cute little hats from Saks. You could always count on their being snuggly outfitted in some fine, black velvet caps with a simple string of pearls from at least *Joseph* Magnin. But look

17

at them now! They all want to look and act so Goddamn *free*. They do their shopping in Sausalito and on Grant Street now that the beatniks have been driven out by the narcs and slick Italians with fast money. Not that I ever *identified* with those purple-faced winos, for Christ sake—I merely beat them at chess because I could drink more Red Mountain than they could.

I speak as a historian, a recorder of events with a sour stomach. I have no love for memories of the past. Ginsberg and those coffee houses with hungry-looking guitar players never did mean shit to me. *They* never took their drinking seriously. And the fact of the matter is that they got what was coming to them. It's their tough luck if they ran out and got on the road with bums like Kerouac, then came back a few years later with their hair longer and fucking marijuana up their asses, shouting Love and Peace and Pot. And still broke as ever.

No sir, I have concentrated on things like the big clock on top of the Ferry Building with Roman numerals and the cars and the trucks with gravel from across the Bay Bridge that buzz by while I plunge ahead in my trusty Plymouth decked out to look like a narco's car. Cables, concrete and congestion, these are the things that matter! Don't give me that fag's "Baghdad-by-the-Bay" bit.

Right about now my stomach reminds me of my clients sitting in the dingy waiting room of the Legal Aid Society at Fourteenth and Fruitvale in the slums of East Oakland. It's already fifteen to nine. Already they're waiting to devour me as they have each day for the past twelve months.

I drive fast, but I am extremely careful. In twenty years of driving—I am thirty-three, the same age as Jesus when he died—I have never had an accident with another car. True, I have rolled three cars on three different occasions, but those were Acts of God, as we lawyers say. And besides, I was drunk. Surely no man would blame me personally for what a foreign substance does to my body. I tell you, I have ulcers. Can you *understand* that? In any event, I do not blame myself.

I turn up the radio full blast . . . "It's Sgt. Pepper's Lonely Hearts Club Band." The boys have finally got themselves a winner. But I can't distinguish the words from the noise of the horns, the skidding brakes, the jangled nerves and my gas-laden belly. Is it a language problem, I ask myself. Or a hearing problem? And how can anyone possibly *understand* even if he does hear?

18

"It's all bullshit," I console myself. "They intentionally make nonsense to sound like poetry so that no one will be able to put them down."

My shrink says, "And is it the same when you hear a new song in Spanish?"

"Fuck, I haven't heard a song in Spanish since I was a kid."

"Oh? You don't like Mexican music?" he stabs it to me.

But I don't have time for that racial crap now. In ten years of therapy the only thing the fucker has wanted to gossip about has been my mother and my ancestry. "Sex and race. It's one and the same hangup." He doesn't seem to understand that my ulcers didn't arrive until I was around eighteen. But he is hung up on ancient history. Moses and Freud really got to him.

I give the beefy, languid guard my quarter for the toll. I rehearse out loud the questions which I'll put to my client this afternoon when I get the annulment for Mrs. Willey. I put it off as long as I could, but now the time has come. She came into my office six months ago, an old lady with long red hair and decidedly sharp pink fingernails. Mrs. Willey said she wanted to annul her marriage. She didn't want to wait the year for the divorce to be final.

"What's the hurry? Do you want to remarry right away?"

"No, sir. It's just that . . . well, Sheila here wants to . . ."

I looked at Sheila's long fingers. She smiled at me.

"What does *she* have to do with your marriage?" I asked.

They looked at one another. They were clearly embarrassed.

Sheila spoke in a fine second-tenor voice, "You see, Mr. Acosta, I want to have an operation. I've already spoken to a doctor."

I waved my hand. "Wait. Hold it . . . What does that have to do with Mrs. Willey? Isn't *she* the one who wants the divorce?"

"Well, we both do . . . I'm her husband," Sheila said to me.

Sheila, it turned out, was a transsexual. She carefully explained the difference between a transvestite and a transsexual. She even left me some reading material on the subject. And it *was* all set up for her to get rid of the penis. I talked to her doctor and he assured me it was all on the up and up. So today, the first of July, 1967 I'd have their marriage annulled on the grounds of fraud: that is, your honor, Mrs. Harriet Willey was led to believe that she was marrying a man. Now this man is in fact not a man. . . . no, sir, he's not quite a woman either. And also, your honor, the reason we can't ask for a divorce is . . . that's right, sir. Mrs. Willey's

19

a Catholic. If the marriage is annulled, she can remarry.

Fortunately I knew that Judge Kassabian was sitting in the Domestic Relations Department of the Alameda County Superior Court for this month. He had a bum hand, polio; and I'd read his son was a draft dodger from Berkeley. Surely a man like that wouldn't mind a little lie. So what if Mrs. Willey wasn't Catholic? This was an uncontested matter. A one-party law suit. No one would know the difference. No one would cross-examine her.

These uncontested matters have been my specialty for a year now. I have over 100 default divorce clients. They're all the same. Just a series of ten questions, ten answers, all well-rehearsed. Everything goes without a hitch. The judges merely wait for my final question to the corroborating witness:

"And you actually saw Mr. Jones strike Mrs. Jones, is that a fact?"

Once the lie is put before the court, the divorce is granted. Just like that. I have won every single case. And now the poor old woman with the cane can apply for welfare assistance for her kids . . . which is all she wanted in the first place. She hasn't seen her old man in five years, but the social worker told her she couldn't apply unless she filed for a divorce first. This social worker logic I no longer contest. When I first passed my Bar I *tried* to obey the law. But that was twelve months ago. Now I simply ask a few questions and my secretary does the rest.

And yet my stomach aches and my heart burns each day as I park behind the drab grey building which houses the numerous Poverty Program offices of the Fruitvale Service Center. We are in the heart of the Oakland Poverty Program's *target area* where so-called organizers and scumbagged legal aiders such as myself are helping the poor, the downtrodden and the lonely. We have employment offices that can't find jobs for the poor saps; training programs for the so-called black and brown people who know damn well they'll never get more than the two bucks an hour they get for training in the first place. We even help people with immigration problems. Mexicans who've been here longer than LBJ himself. But only if the issues aren't too complicated, for after all, we aren't specialists. We're just overburdened, mealy-mouthed, chickenshit lawyers who wouldn't know what the hell to do with a real case if our licenses depended on it. Don't get me wrong, we have the right motives. Our hearts are in the right place. It's just that we aren't competent. We haven't the guts to really take them on. In point of fact, we aren't lawyers, we are simply counselors of old women. We listen to their tales because we have a mandate from Congress . . . and a pretty good salary to boot.

As I enter the run-down building I see them in the cold waiting room with linoleum floors: five unkempt women with bloody noses and black eyes from the old man's weekend drunk. They sit stiffly and pretend to read a *Life* or a *Time*. At this point they're only potential clients. Applicants. First they must prove to my satisfaction that they cannot afford to hire their own private attorney, whatever their problem might be. The government guidelines clearly specify the requirements before they can obtain my free legal counsel. If they earn more than $400 a month for a family of four, then LBJ says they must hire their own lawyer.

You're damn tootin' ol LB ain't gonna take no money from the members of the Bar. Why they'd just go around suin' anybody they didn't like if we didn't have *some* conditions. And so, when we Legal Aid lawyers don't want a case, when the problem is one that we aren't accustomed to dealing with, if it's something we'd actually have to study for and fight about, why, I'm sorry ma'am, but I don't make the rules, I just work here . . . I understand you're in a state of bankruptcy, but still, what with your welfare and your husband's pay check, you just earn too much to qualify for our services. . . . Next!

"But if I had the money I wouldn't be trying to get me a discharge in bankruptcy," they cry out.

And the ones with tears and bruises beg me to help them get rid of their old men. "I already asked two lawyers to get me a TRO and they wants 300 even *before* they go to court."

But didn't the lawyers tell you the court would order your husband to pay for it?" I shout back, my heart pounding.

"Yes, sir. But Mr. Morgan, he done said a court order don't pay the rent. . . . Can't you please just get me a little TRO so's he won't be botherin' me and the children no more?"

They know the lingo of the domestic relations court as well as ex-cons know their criminal law. The first time one fat old lady asked me to get her a TRO I thought it was some ghetto euphemism for a sanitary napkin. My secretary had to tell me it meant temporary restraining order.

And so on Monday mornings like today they come and cry out to me with their hair still matted, their tits still hanging and their grubby, happy kids sliding on the linoleum floors. They are oblivious to my sour stomach and the acid which drips into my chest.

"How in God's name do they expect me to think?" I always demand of my secretary who has done all my thinking for me for twelve months. When the building is filled to capacity, all of us just fighting away against the poverty in the target area, I turn to Pauline for wisdom. She is fifty-seven, a sweet lady with "female" problems who is constantly under the doctor's care and the most gentle and understanding woman I have ever known except for my *Guelita*. From the first day I walked into this building, ready to take on the enemy our president so clearly described in his first State of the Union address, right from the start she has coddled me, burped me, protected me and preserved me for the serious work—the heavy research, which I just haven't quite gotten around to doing yet.

It is Pauline who got a map for me and drew the line from Fourteenth and Fruitvale right up to the front doorstep of the courthouse. She told me where to park, how to fill out my expense voucher, how to prepare a divorce complaint, who the friendly judges were, what clerk one could ask favors of and, most important, what rules one could break. And above all, she is the one who tells prospective clients, "I'm sorry, dear, but Mr. Acosta is just too busy to help you with your TRO. Why don't you just tell your brother to talk to your husband? Or tell him to call me up next time he comes around the house. I'll give him a piece of my mind."

What most people don't understand about lawyers is that they're all scared shitless to actually fight with one another. You see a TRO, unlike an uncontested divorce, requires the *presence* of the opposing party. Unless the drunkard is before the judge, in open court, there isn't much sense in ordering him to stay away from the house and quit beating up on his old lady. All he'd have to say if they caught him is, "I didn't know. No one told me I wasn't supposed to come home anymore."

So in practical terms this means the old man will more than likely show up in court with some private lawyer. Yeh, one of those rich guys with offices downtown near the courthouse. They just love to get ahold of Legal Aid lawyers with our blue suits from Macy's and black ties. Can you just imagine me having to argue with one of those guys? They never even taught me how to cross-examine hostile witnesses in the sleazy night school I attended. And do you think the silver-haired judges come to our assistance? Shit, they too are members of the local Bar. They despise us as much as anyone else. We are socialist creeps, incompetents who know nothing about a hard-earned dollar. For Christ sake, we *give* free legal advice.

On occasion, some of us do argue, some of us do give them

a battle. We actually file Answers to Complaints, can you imagine? And the *private* lawyers with blue silk suits and nicely shined loafers, golden Schaeffer pens, delivery boys, and messenger services at their command, they scream at us, they make us wait on the line until they finish wrapping up some million-dollar insurance claim, and then they caustically warn the lily-livered Legal Aid communist, "Stalling isn't going to help Billy Joe."

They always refer to my clients by their first names. "So what did you file an answer for? He's going to pay for that furniture or else."

"Or else what?" I ask quietly.

"I'll have him in court," he shouts at me.

"I know. That's why we filed our answer."

"But what the hell is your defense?"

"I don't know. I'll figure something out. It'll be two years before we get on the docket."

"That's what I mean! You're just stalling."

"Maybe so. But I've got to do something for him. He's my client, for Christ sake. Besides, maybe by the time we get to court he'll have the money to pay off the balance."

His voice changes. He confides in me as a brother. "For God's sake, Acosta. We'll have to prepare for trial. What do you want to go through all that trouble for?"

"It's my job, man. I get paid for doing this."

If the real truth were to be known, LBJ lost out because of men such as myself. We fucked with those private firms until they couldn't take it no more. Once the organized Bar gave up on Lyndon, it was all over for him. They hate his guts for giving me a salary.

Today is Monday morning. I glance at the five women. I *know* they are TRO material. And I know, I can tell from a distance, that all five are beneath the poverty level. The way they sit quietly, not speaking to one another, their thoughts on the beating their husbands gave them Saturday and Sunday. They have the aura of serious clients. Pauline won't be able to get rid of all of them. And how will I be able to make five excuses in a row? Everyone will know I'm faking it. I'll be exposed even before lunch. There is no avoiding it.

But I can't face them. Not today. I turn the corner into the corridor that leads to the toilet before anyone sees me.

The pain in my stomach, the anguish in my neck, the swirling confusion in my poor head all got out of control this weekend. I got into bed at 7:00 P.M. Friday night and remained between those hot sheets with my eyes fixed on my electronic blue Zenith companion until this morning when I kicked Dr. Serbin out of my shower. I got up only to gobble down burnt hamburgers and to tumble to Wing Lee's to take home some tomato-beef chow mein, which I downed with a quart of Pepsi. Only occasionally did I look out the bay window with the red velvet drapes at the rooftops of the old Victorian apartments in the Polk District. You can see the Golden Gate Bridge from my bed, that orange-colored expanse with strings of yellow fog lights, the green water of the Pacific under its belly—it's taken up much of my time. I've written tons of shitty jibberish, love poems to old girlfriends that I never mail, angry letters to the *Chronicle* that remain unpublished, short stories that only bartenders appreciate, all inspired by that fantastic view. Me and my white Olympia have done this for years. But not lately. Not this weekend. I just stayed in bed and hurt like hell waiting for the phone to ring, waiting for a letter, a message, an invitation to a ball . . . anything to stop the angst.

Not that this was an unusual weekend. It was simply more of the same. But the cumulative effect is getting to me. For twelve months now all I have done is stuffed myself, puked wretched collages in the toilet bowl, swallowed 1000 tranquilizers without water, stared at the idiot-box, coddled myself, and watched the snakes grow larger inside my head while waiting for the clockhand to turn. For twelve months now, since I first began the practice of law, since I became an attorney, a man who speak for others, a counselor at law who has the power to address the court, that's right, a *big* man, a mature person who helps others in distress—for approximately 365 days *time* has been nothing but a never-ending experience that meets me in the morning just like it left me off the night before. No longer am I the clear-headed mathematician of my college years. I used to have the answers; and if I didn't, I could always turn to the back of the book or ask Professor Blackburn at Wednesday morning's advanced algebra class.

For a year now, my only conscious concern has been the pain in my stomach, the arguments of Dr. Serbin, and the schedules of the television shows. I know them all by heart. I can quote every single fucking show on Channels 2, 4, 5, 7, and, you won't believe it, even on the educational station, Channel 9. I am the world's only living *T.V. Guide*, that's *really* what I am.

And they want *me* to counsel them!

No, not today. I just can't face those five fat TRO's under these conditions. Pauline will just have to deal with them, I whisper to myself as I duck into the toilet. If they even see me, their expectations will increase. Things are bad enough for these poor suckers without having to cry over me.

Dr. Serbin squeezes into the green-walled toilet with me. "Oh, of course, you can't give them any false hope. After all, you're just a little brown Mexican boy."

I ignore him. I lock the door. I stand above the familiar white bowl. "God, why don't we have a phone in here." I lower my head for the third time this morning. "If I could just call her from in here, she'd send them away. They could come back tomorrow when Burt Danziger is on duty."

I struggle, I push with my diaphragm at the refuse in my gut. But only rancid, hot air blows . . . the dry heaves! My stomach burns with acid, hot sauce, sawdust hamburgers, Chinese curry, wars and rumors of wars.

I double my fist and strike my belly . . . and this time it comes. The designs of curdled milk and scrambled eggs with ketchup are a sight, a work of genius. I ponder the fluid patterns of my rejections and consider the potential for art. Dali could do something with this, I'm sure. Perhaps I should write to him.

But wait. "Good God, I didn't use any ketchup!"

I strain to puke more. I want to be certain. Positive. Sure enough, there it is again. I think of taking a specimen. Maybe I could put a drop or two in the vial of pills I have in my pocket. But why bother? I *know* it's not ketchup.

"It's blood, God damn it! *Blood,* do you hear?" I scream at my shrink. But of course when I have positive proof, direct evidence such as this, my psychiatrist is busy with some other nut.

"Look at it, you Jew bastard and then tell me it's all in my head!"

I cough one more time just for good measure. The blood floats on top of the scrambled confusion like Eggs Benedict. I stare at it for a long time. It is the best proof I've had in years and I never want to forget it. Now when my friends ask I can tell them what the source of my problems is. I'm tired of saying, "Oh, it's just personal problems, you know." God, if I just had some color film, I would be able to corroborate my testimony. But fuck it, they'll just have to take my word for it. I fix it in my mind forever and then I hurry to my office around the back.

No one sees my arrival. My heart is in a flutter. The bitterness of the green bile is in my mouth. I close the door behind me, and am surprised to see the office is dark. Pauline always lights the office, turns on the heat or the air conditioner when she brings in my cup of hot coffee before my arrival. A glance at my huge, cluttered desk tells me something is definitely wrong. Pauline always straightens my papers out, puts the manila folders with the files for the daily appointments on the right hand corner before I get here. And the fancy mug she gave me, the one with the Chinese red designs, still sits with a finger of cold coffee from last Friday. I pick it up to test for heat. Sure enough, it hasn't even been rinsed.

"Pauline!" The door between our offices is shut. "Pauline," I call in desperation, reaching for the knob. I open the door and my pounding heart stops cold when I see an empty, darkened office. Nothing but business machines and the grey filing cabinets with all our secret information on the husbands of the TRO's.

"Pauline. Are you here?" I call out to the emptiness. In twelve months the grey-haired lady with brown, elastic stockings for her varicose veins has never failed me. She always schedules her doctors appointments on my day off. She's always taken her vacation when I've taken mine. And now when I need her most, she is absent.

I rush into the office next to hers. A long-haired law student from Boalt Hall is doing my serious research.

"You know where Pauline is?" I blurt out agitated.

He looks at me with languid, blue eyes. "Haven't you heard?"

"Heard what? What's up?" I scream at him. Already I blame him.

He looks downcast, his face in the books before him. "She . . . uh, passed away."

"What do you mean?"

"She died. Saturday. Of cancer."

"Cancer? What do you mean? She had . . . she said she had female problems." I lean on the desk for support. My head is exploding. The electrical pills set off the dynamite.

"The funeral's this afternoon. Fike left a message for you."

He hands me a pink pad. The director of the Legal Aid Society of Alameda County, Tom Fike informs me of her death, the funeral, and suggests I cancel my court appointments for the day. I finger it carefully, check the signature and read it three times.

I quietly say to the law student, "Do me a favor and tell those women outside . . ."

"I already did."

"What? Then why are they still out there?"

"They said they'd wait to see if some other lawyer might be able to help them," he says weakly.

"But the others won't be in till this afternoon!" I scream.

"I know, I told them," he says coolly. "They said they'd wait anyway. They all want a TRO."

"God damn it! I knew it!"

As I start to exit, he asks me, "Want some coffee?"

"Jesus, I'll need more than that," and I stumble out the door.

I am in my purple office, at my large, brown desk. With my chin in cupped hands, my insignificant pig eyes survey the walls of books, periodicals, law journals, and tan filing cabinets with the case histories of my innumerable clients, all under a flood of faded, fluorescent white light. My stomach churns and my chest burns. I stuff three chalk Rolaids in my mouth. My huge body is a massive quivering nerve that shakes inside the dark blue Macy's suit my father gave me when I graduated from law school a year ago.

The green telephone rings. Fifteen different numbers, and it is *mine* that lights up! I am electrocuted. It rrrings again. "Probably Mrs. Willey," I think. It rrrrrings again. Traumatized, I stare at it. And again! I detest it, that green machine! I dare it to continue. Rrrrrrrrrrring. "Keep on, you son of a bitch!" Seven times the lesbian calls to me and seven times I challenge it. When it is silenced, I am aware of my singular presence in the room with the purple rugs and the stained walnut walls. It is the first time in my entire life I've refused to pick up a ringing phone. I've even answered the phone when I've been on top of a woman. Anytime you knock on my door, I answer. Doesn't matter what time it is. Write me a letter, give me a call, and you can be sure I'll be there. I've always worried that some day I'll get a call from some smart-assed disc jockey with a million dollars for me and I'll be out. So this is the first time for me. I who am so punctual, never late; I who never missed a single day of school throughout my childhood education, who took every test, kept every appointment, I now remove the telephone from the hook and enjoy my self-indulgence.

My shrink sits on the soft chair in the corner, under the framed Bar license. "Don't worry, they'll live without you."

"Ah, shit! You miss the point."

I reach into my glass-topped desk and take out my reserve pills. I keep the little blue jobs, the Stelazine, in the bathroom of my apartment. In the bedroom, next to the bed by the bay window, I usually have another handful. In case I have an accident on the freeway, I naturally carry a vial full of Valium in the glove box. And of course I always have several in my pocket and a paper-clip box filled with both kinds in my desk. I see no need in taking unnecessary chances. Anxiety attacks come in strange places and at unusual times.

I swallow two, one of each. An upper and a downer to even things out. My shrink observes. "It's the same problem. You just can't be comfortable with the bigness."

"Ah, fuck off!"

He continues to bubble and to babble, but I no longer listen. The light is fading fast. He mumbles and he rumbles but I am impervious.

I have sat at this slick desk for twelve months now. Twelve months of divorces, TRO's, wage attachments, bankruptcies, repossessed cars and furniture, evictions and welfare recipients. How many times have those black faces, those brown legs, those Okie accents sat in front of me and stared at my red $567 IBM typewriter?

Who are these pallid faces with rotting teeth, hair in rolls, scarves around their chins, who sit in my plush, purple office with all the books in the world at my disposal? And why do they have dozens of such seemingly happy, noisy kids? Must they always have good reasons for not paying Sears or Beneficial Finance? Just once can't they say they blew it on booze? Am I really supposed to believe they actually live on $268 a month for a family of four in the year the Beatles made a million? Doesn't LBJ know that Watts burned in '65? That Detroit rioted in '66? That the Panthers started carrying guns in '67? Am I to prevent all this with a carbon copy of a court order that compels a Negro janitor to pay child support for his nine kids? Does anyone seriously believe I can battle Governor Reagan and his Welfare Department even with my fancy $567 red IBM? Do you think our Xerox machine will save Sammy from the draft? Or that our new set of Witkin law books will really help turn the tide in our battle against poverty, powdered milk and overdrawn checks?

Yes, for twelve months I have seen their frightened eyes, that look of desperation that only hungry people carry with them to their lawyer's office. Some even bring babies in their arms and pull the tit out for the kid right in front of me while I write out all the relevant information. And after they tell me their sad tales, show me the tattered contracts with coffee stains, while they sit and sigh and gaze into the deep purple of my rugs, I call the piggish creditors at Household Finance and tell them I represent Mrs. Sanchez, that I'm with the Legal Aid Society.

That gives them the message right away. They know I have the time to deal with them. And right away they laugh at me for even suggesting they reinstate her loan or call off the sheriff with the repossession papers. And when I insist, they curse me for even suggesting that it's impossible for her to make up the back payments because she had to use the money to fix the toilet which had overflowed over the hardwood floors of her two bedroom house for the nine children and three adults . . . and why doesn't she get the landlord to fix it? Well, because she didn't pay the rent; anyway, he wants her to move out . . . so why doesn't she move? Why doesn't she get the Welfare people to give her supplemental aid? . . . Well, you see, her social worker is mad at her . . . seems they found a man living there and they've cut her off until she makes up for those two months she received while this man . . . no, buddy she's not a prostitute. He happened to be a cousin from Mexico without papers. Yes, a wetback and he can't get a job.

You'll take the car back? . . . Forget the back payments? . . . Oh, then you'll sell it and she'll only owe the deficiency? . . . But what'll she do for a car in the meantime? How will she get her kids to school? She has to drive her cousin around to look for a job . . . I know you're not a social worker. I know you're not in this thing for charity, God damn it! But she can't do without it. Can you understand that . . . sir? Hello?

They hang up on me. All the time they crash the bastard into my face because they realize I'll just keep begging all afternoon. This is what I must regurgitate for an hour after Mrs. Sanchez leaves with the bundled, blackheaded kid asleep in her arms. But the worst is the horror of the look in her eyes as she sits quietly while I beg for an extension of time. What has caused me numerous sleepless nights, pains in my legs, raw nerves at my neck; what has been the absolute worst of it all is the sleepy yet knowledgeable look she gives to me when I'm on the phone, the way she *notices* my red $567 IBM typewriter on my mahogany desk . . . that I cannot handle.

The Valium and the Stelazine begin to take hold. The slight buzzing at the base of my neck goes into action.

On my wall hangs the biggest trophy of them all. A scroll with fancy lettering. Signed by the chief justice himself. This is the talisman that permits me to counsel these tired, lonely people. This is the very thing that gives me the power to collect fat checks for services rendered, to be employed rather than hired. It is the emblem of my title: An Attorney and Counselor At Law! Yes, with that number there on the wall I can address the court from the counsel table. I will be heard, under order of the chief justice, is that clear? I can make motions, requests, and even demands from the superior court with that little piece of brittle paper.

Even now while they bury Pauline I think not of her death but of the dimness in my mind. I am not a hypocrite. I know that I didn't really appreciate her. Christmas of 1966, last year, I didn't even buy her a gift. I never even said to her how much I appreciated her, depended on her or liked her. But it is too late now. I'll not be a party to tears for the dead, they have enough problems as it is without having to be concerned with the pain in my stomach. And the truth of the matter is that death is a mystery to me. I have no opinion on the subject.

I only know that I can't continue. The improbable has now become the impossible. Without the lady to fill my cup and shut the door to those TRO's I can no longer put up the pretense that I am a lawyer. It should be clear to you by now that I am a mere pretender. I simply don't care about their bloody noses anymore.

I get up from the desk. I walk to the wall. I stare at the glass-encased license for the last time. Charlie Fisher, a fat artist friend from Trader JJ's, constructed the walnut-stained frame after I passed the Bar. Because I had flunked the exam the first time around in the summer of 1965, all my friends had waited with great anticipation for the results of the second exam in June of 1966. They were sorely disappointed when I brought the proof of my success into the bar. I demanded that Sal (the crafty Sicilian owner of the joint at Polk & Jackson Streets where I had been studying for my exams over pitchers of draft beer) hang it behind the bar over the cash register. He refused and told me that I should be proud. "How many guys like you do you know that are lawyers?" he asked me with one of those short, brown Toscana cigars between his teeth.

"What do you mean, 'like me'?"

"Ah, don't play cute. You know what I mean. Shit, your old man would kick your ass if you did something like that, Osc."

Charlie looked it over carefully, brought me a drink and said, "Hey, Osc, if you want, I'll frame it for you. I'll make it real neat."

And so he did. The fat artist from Bimidji who still talks in the hep style of the early fifties—as much as a Republican banker's son can—he framed it for me without charge and we celebrated with fried chicken and barbequed spare ribs from Wing Lee's.

But that was long ago. Now the time has come for me to reveal my true feelings. A man must expose himself totally, in all his shame, if he is to share in the true glory. The fact of the matter is that I care not one wit for the oath of my office. I don't give one rat's ass *what* the Code of Ethics says. I'm going to dump all my 150 divorce clients just like that. Mrs. Willey will simply have to find some other expert on transsexuals. My single, utmost concern is to get those fucking ants out of my stomach.

I remove my license from the nail on the wall and kiss it goodbye . . . I dump it in the wastepaper basket and my escape begins.

I grab the phone and dial the Alameda County Superior Court. Mr. Simpson, a large-sized midget with a bum leg who showed me the ropes around the Domestic Relations Department when I first began, answers my call.

"Mr. Acosta, how are you? I see you're on this afternoon."

"That's what I'm calling about," I say.

"Something wrong?"

"Would you please tell Judge Kassabian to take the Willey matter off calendar."

"Sure, but . . ."

"Don't worry, Fred. It's an uncontested matter. It'll be reset."

"Sure thing . . . uh, are you ill?"

"I'm okay. It's my secretary."

"Pauline?"

"Yeh . . . she died this morning."

I hang up the phone and immediately dial the main office of the Alameda County Legal Aid Society.

"Tom? It's me, Oscar." Tom is my Irish-Catholic boss who thought he was doing me a big favor by giving me my first job as a lawyer.

"Yeh, man. Did you get my note?" he speaks like a pall bearer.

"I've cancelled my appointments and court appearances."

"Didn't make it to the funeral, eh?"

"I'm taking off right now."

"It's already over with, man. We buried her at ten."

"No. Look, I'm leaving the office."

"What do you mean? Want a day off?"

"No, man. I'm splitting. Tell Burt he'll have to take over my cases."

"Hey, wait a bit . . . listen, why don't you come over . . . let's have lunch." His voice sounds like a young girl who is being dumped.

"Lunch? Are you kidding?"

He chuckles. "All right, man. I'll spring for it."

"Jesus! Just tell Burt to handle it."

"Hey, Oscar!" And then his voice drops to a baritone, a boss.

"You can't simply walk out. The Bar would really frown on us just dropping a case load like you've got."

"Well, fuck it. Tell them I'm not a lawyer anymore. They can have their license back. It's in my wastepaper basket."

I hang up in his face. Another first for me. When women shit on me, when filthy scum creditors fuck with my head, when hotshot lawyers from Harvard or Hastings overpower me with their superior knowledge, I take it all. I have never hung up a telephone on anyone until today.

Dr. Serbin stands by the bookshelf and says, "Perhaps it's a sign of maturity."

"Or rudeness," I reply.

Now I have cleared the road and the coast is clear. I quickly dump the contents of my center drawer into my black briefcase. Pencils and felt tip pens, invitations to political parties, applications for membership in the National Lawyers' Guild, unanswered letters and telephone messages which I know I'll get to now that I'm free, and seven packages of Juicy Fruit. (I've always had a fear of bad breath. I chew the hell out of it before I talk to a client and sometimes I stuff a whole pack in my mouth before we go to the counsel table at the courthouse.)

I take the paper-clip box full of Stelazine and finger it. When I first began with Dr. William Serbin he was only an intern at Mt. Zion hospital near Divisadero, in what used to be the Fillmore District where all the niggers lived until they drove them out to make room for the white people, the Catholic Church and some rich Japs. A girl from St. Louis suggested I visit Mt. Zion to see if they might have a cure for my ulcers. The first time I applied they told me I wasn't sick enough to get on their emergency list and instead gave me a list of names of various private psychiatrists in San Francisco.

I went to see a Dr. Rubenstein three times at twenty-five bucks a throw and spent the entire time arguing about the cost of his services. I returned to Mt. Zion in the fall of 1957. This time I told them I had an unexplainable urge to kill my mother with the same ice-hooks she'd used to beat me with when I was seven years old. They sent me immediately to see one of their young interns and I told him—Dr. Serbin—that I had this thing about paying cold cash for a doctor's advice. He told me it was none of his concern. That was a matter I'd have to take up with the girls downstairs in the cashier's office. I never paid them a dime.

Dr. Serbin interrupts. "You'll notice that was in 1958, not '57. I am now in private practice."

"Ah, for Christ sake. Just think, you'll get honorable mention in the numerous books they'll write about me when I'm famous."

In any event, in 1958 he ordered me to take one (1) pill per day. The following year he had the pharmacist put on the label: "Take As Needed." Now, some ten years later, I am on a steady diet of what big blond Larry Otterness, a psychiatrist friend of Charlie's, has told me are, quite simply, "crazy pills." He said, "I give them only to my really crazy patients." These doctors sure know how to make a guy feel good. Yes, I take Stelazine, the strongest of the bunch, five mg. a swallow and I suck on them like candy all day long. And still my stomach hurts.

I write Burt, my baldheaded partner, a note:

> B . . . I'm splitting. All I have is yours. I'm leaving you this little box of helpers. If you stay here much longer, you'll need them.

Chapter Three

I hurry out the back and escape into the traffic without any confrontations. I turn on the radio full blast. An outrageous organ pumps out a spooky religious hymn . . . "A Whiter Shade Of Pale"? I'm caught up in a fog full of crazy pills. The man says something about blessed virgins and cartwheels cross the floor. Do I *hear* those words? I admit I cannot understand them. But is he really saying those things? Jesus, maybe I overdid it.

"And of course there's Pauline to consider," my shrink says from the back seat.

"Oh, fuck off. This is serious," I tell him in my most serious tone, while my rib cage is strapped with hot cords. I strain to hear every word that Moose on KYA tells me are being sung by a deep mystery called Procol Harum. The song moves me deeply. It reminds me of Luther's "A Mighty Fortress Is Our God." I can't say I'm a religious person, but what with the Stelazine and the blood in the toilet, I guess you might say I feel spiritual at the present.

35

I look up just the instant before my green Plymouth zooms close by a huge concrete post. The fog and the mist of the bay wet the Broadway cut-off and I twist the wheel against a skid. The rear end jackknifes a tango step. I cut it back into the railing and when it rolls straight I realize I've been in a trance for some time. I have no memory of paying the toll or driving across the Bay Bridge.

"For Christ sake! What is this?"

My shrink says, "What? You mean the self-hypnosis? It's very common."

Naturally there's nothing unusual about my condition. All my symptoms have been common to every man for years now. He refuses to permit me the satisfaction of uniqueness. I look into the rear view mirror. My eyes sparkle red. Holy Mary, Mother of God! He winks at me. Did you see that? The crazy bastard actually winked at me. What kind of shit is this?

I pull over at a ma and pa liquor store across the street from City Lights Bookstore, a hangout for snivelling intellectuals and runaway teenyboppers out for a score. As soon as I get back in the car I take a slug of Old Fitzgerald. I almost always drink scotch, but when you want to get serious about drinking you have to jump into some heavy shit and fuck the hangover. Firewater brings out the real brownness of this buffalo.

I press on the pedal and zoom through the tunnel under the hill. The yellow tile inside the enclosure cuts off the radio. It would be two years before Herb Caen would raise bread for an electrical job that would permit him to hear Russ Hodges say his famous Bye-Bye Baby-bit while inside the three-block-long tunnel. On July the first, 1967, I still have to suffer along with the rest of the uninformed. And as I come out at the west end the radio is roaring "A Whiter Shade Of Pale" once again.

"I'm into a fucking time tunnel," I bang my fist on the steering wheel and laugh with the abandon of madness. I swallow more of the high-class whiskey and shake my head. "It's not enough. I need something stronger," I speak audibly to myself.

Dr. Serbin puts it to me. "You mean you're not going to go home and watch T.V.? *Edge Of Night* comes on at 2:30, you know."

"Shit, who needs T.V.? I'm on the loose, can't you see?"

I cruise her down into the Polk District where Chinese women with brown stockings are taking little steps into the markets and fancy-assed fags are selling flowers on the corners to young girls in leather and crocheted ponchos. I remember that Charlie told me his sister, Cynthia had said that Ted Casey, the fat seaman from Brooklyn, was now selling drugs.

"Just what I need," I say to no one as I drive up Sutter to his apartment. I haven't seen him or his old lady, Alice, for nearly a year . . .

Three years ago, in the fall of 1964 I had mononucleosis, a disease of the blood that knocks you flat on your ass for months. It's a student's disease that arises in the season of ennui when you have no place to go. I lay perfectly still for five weeks in my apartment on Hyde Street looking out the bay window at the Golden Gate Bridge. No one, not one single person visited me. Desperate for a voice other than that of my shrink, I called Charlie Fisher. After the usual chit-chat he told me his sister Cynthia was moving into San Francisco. She was tired of Minnesota and had been squandering her trust fund in Europe for some time.

The next morning I finally got up, summoned all my strength, and walked a step at a time like the old Chinese ladies to the corner for a bowl of Wing Lee's won-ton soup. Upon returning to my apartment at 1515 Hyde Street, I looked uselessly in my mail box. I noticed a new name on the box next to mine . . . C.K. Fisher. A few days before I thought I'd heard someone moving into the apartment building. And Charlie's middle initial was K. But of course it was just a coincidence. Charlie and his wife Donna lived three blocks down, across the street from Trader JJ's. But what the hell, it would be an excuse to start a conversation—five weeks without company get to even the strongest. I dragged my feet one at a time up the stairs and knocked on the door.

A young, short-haired blonde in jeans and a simple tee shirt opened the door. I asked innocently, "Say, are you Charlie's sister?"

"How'd you know?" She spoke with a twang, a nasal midwestern accent.

"Really? Jesus, I was kidding."

Because Charlie was a Republican, a banker's son with a huge trust fund, an artist without pretensions of greatness who simply liked to paint canvases of zoftig nudes and slashed-faced, pink rabbits with blood dripping from their jaws, I assumed that Cynthia would be as square as he. Five minutes after I walked into her apartment—it was a duplicate of my one-room job, but without the view of the bay—I smelled an odor that I had never smelled before. It had a touch of sin, a musky odor of sensuality that I knew couldn't be anything to eat.

I smoked marijuana for the first time in my life with Cynthia. She, too, was an artist. But she was crazier than Charlie would ever be. While we drifted into the fog of my first joint on a cloudy

San Francisco afternoon, she showed me drawings of Egyptian men with the bodies of dogs on roller-skates coasting down pyramids of chocolate ice-cream. My head split while I tried to "understand" her art. I wanted to say *something*. But all that I could muster was a "Jesus, what is this?"

"If you really want to get into it . . . whyn't you try this?"

I sat on the soft chair and looked up at her nice, small tits, the blue eyes of a nasty little girl handing me some white capsule. Of course I wanted to fuck her right then and there. But she was Charlie's sister, for Christ sake.

"What is it?" I asked. What I knew about drugs in those days you could write on your thumb.

"LSD," she said.

"What'll it do?"

"It's really something. I've taken it twice."

"Yeh, but what's it *do*?"

"Well . . . it helps you to understand. To see things. Shit, you just have to try it . . . unless you're scared," she put it to me.

Thirty minutes after I swallowed it with soda water, my neck was gripped with the most excruciating pain I've ever experienced. The devil took me by the back of the neck and I regressed to my fifth birthday and demanded an extra scoop of strawberry ice-cream from my mother, who was sitting where Cynthia had been. I fell to the floor at the age of two when my baby legs gave out from under me. My mother just told me not to worry. I curled up in my old fetus position and cried for my mother's breast, but she would have none of it. "You'll come out of it, Oscar. Just don't fight it," she said to me.

When I could no longer see the light because of the darkness of her womb, I shook it off, crawled into a space ship, shot out of the darkness and asked Cynthia if she wanted to go for a ride.

"Jesus Christ, Oscar. You've had me on your trip for two hours. Don't be such an egotist."

Suddenly I looked up and everything seemed perfectly natural. I said to her, "Would you believe that I now understand everything there is to know of cubism? Picasso just explained it all to me. And your drawings are fucking super."

She sat across the room from me as we politely drank some Irish tea she'd brewed with cinnamon and honey. With her arms draped over that green chair she'd gotten from the Salvation Army out on Geary Street, Jackie Kennedy told me she'd come into town with two girl friends from Minnesota to join the Zen church in

Jap Town, but that she hadn't gotten around to it since she'd received a post card from Bob Dylan, a friend whom they'd palled around with in school. I wasn't too impressed because I was on acid and also because I hadn't heard of Bob Dylan at the time. She showed me a paper poster announcing a concert he was to give at the Masonic Auditorium that winter. He'd scrawled some note on it and an invitation to get together after the Sunday night gig. The postscript told her to "try this number I've scotch-taped above. Be cool, fool."

When I looked at myself in the full-length mirror on her closet door I was surprised to see that the drug had made the hair on my otherwise smooth arms grow green and long. "Look, Cynth, I'm the Wolfman," I joshed. I turned to see Teddy Roosevelt riding his horse up San Juan Hill. "Is that a carrot or a stick you got in your mouth?" he asked me. I turned to face my image in the mirror and I saw the green hair coming out gently, like a growing flow of green weeds. My face was now completely covered with hair. Not just a beard, God damn it; I mean my entire body was that of the green Wolfman, good ol' Lon Chaney, the green son of a bitch that used to scare the shit out of me at the Saturday night movies.

Just about then we heard a knock on the door. Instant fear. Cops? Doctors with white jackets? Another Chinese Tong war? Just who in God's name would be visiting at this hour when I'm about ready to get into the heavy sex talk with Debbie Reynolds?

One girl with short red hair, Mary. One blonde with fine long legs, Alice. One seven-foot-tall gorilla named Hewey who broke every bone in my hand. They say he was once the heavyweight champ of Ireland and that he used to spar with Joe Louis. A short, stubby gruff with a brown camel's hair sport coat from Hong Kong.

Cynthia told me the shorter guy's name was Ted Casey and right from the start he wanted to know who I was. And what the fuck was I doing taking drugs if I was going to be a lawyer. I didn't pay him too much attention because I was more involved in watching the fine ship of Alice's ass sway with the beat of Dylan's "Like A Rolling Stone." In any event, Ted and Hewey were seamen from Brooklyn waiting for a ship. The girls had picked them up at some bar down by the Embarcadero the day before, and if I simply bided my time I'd have all three of them to myself come the weekend.

The girls promised to bring me hot soup and other goodies to get over my mono. I didn't even say goodbye to the two toughs when I went back to my bed by the bay window. I only tried marijuana a few times after that during the next three years and I swore I'd never become the green Wolfman again. I ended up becoming good friends with both Alice and Cynthia when I realized I could never get the bastard up to fuck women who have treated me as kindly as they did for the next month while I got over mono.

I ran into Ted and Alice occasionally at Cynthia's place over the next two years, and then I got in the habit of stopping at their pad on Sutter Street on my way to Dr. Serbin's office. "What the fuck you want to go see him for?" The pudgy, black Irishman from Brooklyn would throw it in my face every time. He'd tighten his muscles, suck in his belly and make like Rocky Marciano. "See this?" He'd grab his cock and pull up the crotch until Alice would say something like, "Oh, Ted, you're going to wrinkle your pants. I *just* got them out of the cleaner's."

They always spoke in tones of exasperation. While I sat and suffered the fucking consequences of my anticipated shrink visit, they'd argue about important matters like why hadn't he taken the garbage out, or why did she have to take that night course at S.F. State? And everytime I tried to explain to Ted what I was going to say to Dr. Serbin, he'd better it with a short story about some broad he fucked in Hong Kong or Bangkok or Tokyo. The man from Brooklyn had seen the world, and what in fuck was the sense in going to college and getting degrees from idiots who had never seen a woman stick a quart-sized bottle of sake in her cunt? He merely laughed when I told him I liked JFK. And when I'd try to explain that I didn't really want to be a lawyer, that I was going to law school just so I could do better than the copy-boy job I had with the *S.F. Examiner* at the time, he would simply walk out of the room. In a word, Ted wasn't interested in anyone else's situation. Particularly the predicaments of a Brown Buffalo who hinted that he secretly yearned for his old lady when he was shipping out to Bangkok.

A year before I puked blood in the toilet, I had asked Ted if he was serious about his indifference to any affairs Alice might have.

"Sure, man. Long's she don't cut my balls. She can do what she wants," he spoke in that Brooklyn-Irish swashbuckle way of his, spitting the words at you as if he had some time clock to follow.

"Are you trying to tell me you wouldn't care if I made it with your old lady?" I was pushing it to him. Of course I knew he was lying through his teeth. Shit, if anyone ever fucked with my old lady—if I *had* one—I'd stick a knife in the bastard's throat so fast . . .

"You? Sure, Osc. If she wants to. Be my guest."

I smiled my best fucking suave Joe Cool look. "We already have."

He just laughed. I had to hurry to keep my appointment with Dr. Serbin so we didn't quite get into it. Three weeks later Charlie told me that Ted said he was going to cut my balls off if he ever caught me in his house again, so I didn't go see them again. Instead, I visited Alice once in a while in my shower room . . .

I ring Ted Casey's buzzer over and over but no one answers. He probably knows it is me and doesn't want to open the door, the fat freak. Just when I need to tell someone, to get some ideas, a little feedback as they say, just when I need advice on the best way one should fire his shrink and the fucker won't open the door! The hell with it! I can do it without that hazy drug anyway. Who needs you, Ted Casey! If you really want to know the truth, I *respect* Alice. But of course an Irishman like you wouldn't understand that.

By the time I reach my shrink's high-class pink office I've finished off the pint of Old Fitzgerald. I know that he has another patient with him. He is a successful doctor—XKE and the whole bit. But it doesn't matter. I'll just put it to him straight. Anyway, he has no receptionist. Nothing but red carpets and plastic flowers in the waiting room. Fuck those magazines, I'm not going to wait.

I bang on the door. I wonder what his patient looks like. In ten years I've never said a word to anyone in the waiting room, anyone in that building with five fucking shrinks, except Dr. Serbin. The door slowly comes ajar. Only his skinny face and tweed coat are visible. I strain to look beyond him, to catch a glimpse of what other nuts look like on that God damn couch of his.

"I've come to tell you I'm leaving," I begin.

In his best supercool tone he offers, "I'm with someone right now."

"I figured that. I just wanted to tell you I'm quitting."

"Can you come back in about two hours?"

This guy is real class. Nothing shakes him. Not even when I had my two nervous breakdowns and got put in the nut ward of S.F. County General out on Potrero, not even then did he bat an eye.

"Two hours? Fuck no. I just want you to know it's cold turkey

41

from now on." My head is just about to blast off my neck.

"Look, Mr. Acosta, why don't you just sit and wait in the lobby. I'll be able to talk to you in . . . half an hour."

Here I am, reeking of whiskey, red in my eye and all the tall, skinny bastard wants to do is talk. I shake my head viciously, with a purpose and say, "I just wanted. . . . Fuck it!"

I turn and walk away from him. After ten years I turn my back on that Jew with his ancient history hangups. I get into the car. I cannot control myself. The laughter of madness clenches my throat. Tears are flowing down my fat cheeks, their wetness is warm. A ghost shivers down my back. But I feel good. I shake it off and go to seek more of that demon rum. There is nothing to stop me now. I have paid all my debts, I have paid all my dues and now nothing remains but the joy of madness. Another wild Indian gone amok.

Chapter Four

I was roaring drunk and decidedly crazy by the time I arrived at Trader JJ's. Surrounded by Russian Hill on the north and Nob Hill on the east, JJ's was caught between the Chinese expansion on one side and the gay liberation on the other. The Chinks and the fags were constantly chipping away at our defense, but through the efforts of hard-core intellectuals, funky artists, tough-minded engineers, humble poets, unpublished writers, drunken lawyers and dropouts of all description, we had managed somehow to keep the joint free of all foreign ideology. Throughout the entire sixties—while under attack by missionaries from the Jehovah's Witnesses and undercover organizers from the Civil Rights movement—we fought hard against peddlers of anxiety, those hustlers with dandruff who'd come into the dive, order a pitcher of draft beer and start to recite their pledges of allegiance to matters that didn't concern us one bit.

JJ's was the only bar in San Francisco where you could drop your pants and run a tab without being 86'd. The only rule of the house was not to disturb either the owner, Sal, or the bartender, Don. If you wanted to become a part of the inner sanctum, then of course you had to share your dirty secrets with them and permit them seconds on whatever strangers you happened to pick up in the dingy, green inn; a rumrunners' hideout before the fire of '06, the oldest bar in the city of sin with cells for Shanghai affairs still operative when I stopped to say goodbye on July first, 1967.

I had consumed another pint of Old Fitzgerald while packing my meagre belongings. I carefully wrapped my collection of Dylan, who by this time had become the only musician worth listening to, my hardcover books on calculus, advanced algebra, and relativity along with the thick books on real property, futures, con law and evidence. I had quit reading fiction in the late fifties as a waste of time, and I was always too broke throughout these years to buy clothes, so I managed to get everything of worth into one carload and took them down to JJ's, where I planned to store them before I continued my journey.

Don, the short, redheaded kid with white tennis shoes was on duty. He constantly scratched at his warts, which he attributed to his so-called "nervous affliction." I called him over to the corner in front of the huge iron safe where I always sat and in a whisper asked him for 100 on my tab and permission to store the junk in the cellar.

"Put the stuff in the cellar with the other shit. But I can't give you that much bread on the tab. Sal will be in at eight," he said in his frog's voice.

"Shit, I can't wait."

"Listen to him, will you?" he said to the others at the bar. It was late afternoon. The cocktail hour had begun when Don opened at noon for these unemployed twirps. There was no sense in hitting *them* up. They were just drinking draft beer and waiting for a score.

"Bread? Osca, *you* want bread?" Maria, the Jewish switchhitter screamed in Billie Holiday tones. She had lived on exactly twenty-five bucks a week for as long as we could all remember. She had absolutely refused to do anything but paint fantastically simple absurdist-primitives and occasionally hustle whatever strangers—male or female—happened to drop in. It was simply inconceivable to this Jew from the Bronx that a person who earned 850 bucks a month would ever have to ask for credit.

"Oh, ho!" Jolly, old fat Ricks perked up. "Got yourself a snatch?" He came up and hovered over me with his usual shit-grinning inquisitiveness, his balding head bent just the right amount to show his concern. He wanted to be *everyone's* partner in crime. He bummed drinks professionally, with class, by catering to everyone's problems when he wasn't working as an extra in the S.F. Opera Co.

"And who's talking to you fucks?" I roared at them. "You know I'm not the sort who likes to have his personal problems bandied about by a bunch of cheap drunks." They all laughed, knowing as they did my most serious defect: the compulsion to tell everyone, including strangers, the story of my life.

"Snatch?" the blackheaded Billie Holiday warmed up. "And just what would Osca do with a snatch, even if he could get one?" She finished off her obscenities with a boisterous laugh, typical of drunken floozies from the Bronx too old to make it on looks.

Maria knew exactly how to cut me down to size. The first night I'd met her in JJ's I was still new to the joint. She was with some redheaded lesbian with a beautiful ass. A big, thick-armed marine sergeant in his dress blues came up and asked me if I wanted to help him with these two broads he'd just picked up. I naturally nearly busted my pants hurrying them into his car. We stopped at a liquor store and Maria asked him for money to get some booze for her pad. Then the redhead hit him for some bread to get some Chinese food. Maria told him to wait in the car and grabbed my hand. The poor sap sat there like a Boy Scout in his dress blues. But instead of walking into the liquor store, Maria pulled me into a telephone booth and put it straight, "Listen, man. I'm broke. Let's dump these creeps."

We ended up at her basement studio under the Chinese laundry, in the same building where Charlie Fisher lived. She fixed me some fine minestrone soup and poured thick, red wine while I flipped my head at the original pop pad, before the world had heard of Campbell Soup Cans and Dick Tracy comics as art. She painted oils of baby flowers, made collages of burnt plastic dolls in wire cages, had posters of Peter Lorre and Sidney Greenstreet in the kitchen, and had drawings of the best twelve ways to fuck in the toilet. From the moment we entered the apartment, she started to act like a Jewish mother. She called me "dear" and removed my coat. She wanted me to be *comfortable*.

When I finished puking in the toilet, I decided to take a bath. It was nearly 3:00 A.M. and I hadn't had a bath in almost twenty-four hours. I filled the tub and after soaping myself down, I fell asleep.

"You son of a bitch!" I awoke to her screams. She was standing over me a woman scorned, her black eyes blazing. "You dirty motherfucker."

"What is it?" I rubbed my eyes.

"You bastard. Falling asleep while I wait for you in bed."

"Bed? . . . Jesus, Maria, I'm sorry . . . I thought you knew."

"Knew? Knew what?" she backed off.

I thought fast with my little limp prick floating in the soap suds. "I don't like to talk about it . . . I had an accident."

"Oh, fuck, Osca . . . that's an old one."

"I know . . . but in my case . . . look." I looked at my wilted penis. "I swear to God that thing hasn't risen in ten years."

"You lying bastard," she said without conviction.

And so we never went to bed. At least not under the covers as lovers do. I passed out on top of her black bedspread, under the red 4×6 oil, as I was to do many times thereafter. Maria became one of the many women friends I always kept around to protect me from the Frisco fog and my dead vine. I never screwed any of them, I just kept them to hear me out.

A couple of years later when I had the first of my serious nervous breakdowns, she drove me to S.F. General and sat in the waiting room, bitching at the attendants until they received me into their arms for a three-day observation period. The very first night I was awakened by some young Puerto Rican shuffling in hospital slippers at 3:00 A.M. singing, "Oh, mama, can this really be the end? To be stuck inside a mobile with the Memphis Blues again." I was so fucking impressed with that kid's line, I actually wrote it on a piece of Kleenex. Years later when I heard Dylan sing it, I figured he must have stolen it from that curly-headed crazy nigger. He repeated it over and over and over until the entire ward started to crack. I told the doctor the next morning I thought I was ready to go home. He made me stay another two days, probably just to teach me a lesson. I called Maria, she picked me up like I knew she would and we drove over to Sausalito and got drunk at the No Name Bar with some fag friends of hers.

After that, Maria never bothered me again, she just told everyone at JJ's about my dead vine.

"Shit, Osca ain't had a snatch since that bird, Mac-a-Who? . . . Since she left him," Maria dug into me. My heart fell into a stomach full of gas. She had mentioned the unmentionable: June MacAdoo. My Frisco broad who had dumped me the year before.

Jose came to my defense. "Well, if he did get one, he'd probably sell her to you, you bitch!" The tall, pimple-faced man was a mystic of classic proportions, a Mexican fag who'd never gotten over catching his mother with some man in a Salinas grape vineyard where he learned all his Catholicism. Although the Polk District was filled with queens, butches and fags, Jose Ramon Lerma was one of the few homosexuals we tolerated at JJ's. Not simply because he had learned to keep the beast in his pockets, but because he was the only artist of the whole bunch of scags that had seriously studied at one time or another under Jack Jefferson at the San Francisco Art Institute. And because Jack had said he was the only one in the area destined for greatness, if the devil didn't get to him first. So we permitted him our holy heterosexual company. Without Jack's recommendation, we'd probably have let Jose starve; but instead, many of us bought him a beer and a Polish sausage when he came in with his paint-splattered cords and brown brogans, broke as ever.

I shouted at Don, "See what you did, you fucking red midget?"

"Who? Me?" He smiled his little boy nastiness. He twinkled his wrinkled green eyes to get even.

"Yes, you. You know better than to let these winos in on a secret."

Ricks hung over me in his bext conspiratorial pose. He whispered, "What's up, O? Don't tell me you're seeing . . . oh, you sly rascal."

He was good, a baldheaded masochist always looking for affection. He even had private names for everyone. I had planned to get it over as soon as possible. I knew that once my friends got a hold of my trauma for that day they'd come down heavy. I wasn't in any mood for our special brand of therapy, the JJ school of attack and conquer when they're down, we were specialists in adding insult to injury whenever possible. I merely shook my head at Ricks.

Don came up to me. "It's your fault, you dumb spic. You know better than to bother me when I'm working on my cross-word puzzle."

Fair enough, I thought. I snapped back to reality. When Maria mentioned that name I thought for a moment I was a goner. No one talked about June MacAdoo in my presence. Jose had introduced me to her the week after I'd taken my first Bar exam in August, 1965. The three of us played pool in the back room. I gave her a ride home and ended up staying in her pad for the next three months. She had skinny legs and an ass that was firm, but not much of a shape. Her tits were small. Her hair was too thin and black and short, like a pageboy, and she had a little pug nose. But that Rumanian lass from South Carolina was the cutest chick I'd ever loved and my only serious affair of the sixties.

The week before I got my results from the bar examiners she

47

woke up one morning and told me she didn't love me anymore. We'd been living at her pad on Polk & Bay Streets two blocks up from The Buena Vista ever since that first night we played pool, so I didn't take her seriously when she poured our morning Japanese tea in bed and told me, "I don't know why, but I've lost it for you."

I just smiled. "You didn't do bad last night."

"I know, dear. But this morning I just don't have it anymore."

After our boiled eggs on the hardwood floor of the yellow and orange lacquered kitchen, I kissed her goodbye and she left for The City of Paris where she worked as an assistant cashier. I had been waiting for three months for the Bar results and getting drunk everyday at JJ's. I figured that if she had supported me for three months, wrapped her skinny, warm legs around my naked body while we listened to Gene Shepherd on KFRC tell us stories about his childhood—I figured that the real reason she hadn't wanted to make love before she left for work that morning was because I had yet to actually set a date for our wedding.

I'd told her numerous times I definitely wanted to marry her. I told her I loved her like a wife. She never did respond. Instead she told me stories about her Jewish grandmother who would die if she knew she was living in sin with a Samoan like me. She didn't once tell me she loved me and she never said a word about the wedding. But I thought what was really bothering her down deep inside was my failure to set the day.

"Shit, I'll buy her a ring the day I get my Bar results," I said out loud as I started on my first drink at 10:00 A.M. I was absolutely positive I'd pass the Bar. I'd never flunked a test in my life. I liked to study. And I was so cocksure of myself that I didn't even take a review course.

Of course that was my downfall. The week after June told me she didn't love me, I got the *small* envelope from the Committee of Bar Examiners. We'd been told by our teachers at San Francisco Law School, the oldest night law school in the state, that if you *passed*, you'd get a large manila envelope with the application; but if you *flunked*, you'd just get a little brown job with your score. I missed it by less than one percentage point.

I cried like a baby for three hours and moved out the next day, after borrowing 100 bucks from June. I never saw her again. Instead I went back to see Dr. Serbin after a two years' absence, studied like hell for three months and took the exam again. And when I passed this time, in June of 1966, it simply no longer mattered. The harm had been done. I just couldn't get over June.

I went outside and started lugging in the cardboard boxes full of my books and records down to the cellar. For twelve years, all through college and law school, I'd been unable to get rid of any printed or written material that in any way whatsoever touched me. I'd kept all my text books, my exams, my notes, schedules of classes, announcements of events, hungry poems written in the dark on scraps of paper, and any other paraphernalia that described me. I was going to make certain that my biographers had all the information they'd need to make a complete report.

Both Ricks and Jose offered to help me carry the stuff. I turned them down because I was broke, and I wouldn't be able to return the favor. I was sweating and my face was covered with dust when I finished. Back upstairs the gang was huddled in the corner making cute remarks about a green animal in a cage that Donna, the wife of an ex-crewmember of *The Enola Gay*, and Russel Tansey, her latest lover, had just brought in.

"Are you going to breastfeed it?" Maria asked.

"Let's not have any of your nasty lip!" Russel, the long-fingered lawyer, addressed the bar. "And you!" He turned to me.

I nodded at my brother, smiled, and seeing an opening, I ordered a pitcher of draft beer.

"You! I'm addressing you, counsel!"

I could see there was no avoiding the arm of the law. Russel had graduated from Hastings, the internationally famous law school that hired only senile experts to teach anyone who didn't have quite the money for a school with real class, like Harvard or Yale. They took out their feelings of inferiority on guys like me who went to some chickenshit night school like S.F. Law School at Post & Polk. He had graduated when I was only a sophomore, and he had just not gotten used to the idea that I, too, was a lawyer.

"What's that beast you got there, Tansey?"

"That, my dear fellow, is an iguana."

"Oscar, meet Greensleaves," Donna said to me. She shoved the monster in my face. An eight inch green lizard that eventually became the mascot of Trader JJ's just stared at me with black, snake eyes. I nodded.

Jose was reeling by now. He had to lean on something in order to stand. "Why are you so mean, Donna? Why do you keep the poor thing locked up?"

The petite lady with the leopard skin pillbox hat pursed her lips, her powdered cheeks accented two blazing green eyes. She put her hands to her hips and screeched, "So you won't get your filthy hands on him!

Ricks roared at that one. He slapped Jose on the back.

"And that goes for you too, Buster," Russel ordered me.

That did it. I immediately guzzled down two glasses of beer. I could see it coming. There was no mistaking where this was all leading to. I'd been through this madness before. A thousand times I'd seen it develop just like on this occasion. Even with the pills, whiskey and beer I could recognize the symptoms. Greensleeves was just a warning.

"Oscar, come here a minute," Russel ordered me over. I just looked at him. "What's this I hear you're leaving? Is that a fact?" my senior brother inquired.

So it was out. My little redheaded prick of a bartender must have told them. Everyone stopped his drinking and waited for my reply. All the booze was no help. My stomach was grumbling and my legs were on fire.

"That's about it . . . I'm splitting this burg . . . leaving it all to you."

There was absolute silence. We could hear the buzz of the fan above the jukebox.

"Big deal!" Maria screamed.

We all broke up. No matter how black things got, you could always count on that lesbian to cheer you up.

I tossed down another fast glass of beer. "Yeh, big deal."

Russel threw in for good measure, "Can't take the pressure, eh? I told you you should have gone to Hastings!"

Jose, my only countryman I'd known in San Francisco came to my defense. "Oh, don't be such a pig, Tansey. You middle-class whore." Jose didn't approve of Russel's new job. He'd just recently been hired by the district attorney's office in Richmond, across the Bay.

I lifted the pitcher to my mouth and swallowed the remaining two glasses without stopping. No single living human on this earth can beat me in a chug-a-lug. I gave an enormous belch and banged it on the bar. "Fill her up, Red Dog!"

I ran into the toilet and puked a barrel of foam. Dark red blotches of blood fizzed along with the suds. It no longer mattered. Standing at the urinal next to the sink, I could see myself in the mirror. I was the original Cro-Magnon Man from the profile. The beast they found in the tar pits was my grandfather. The bastards would have to bring up my little Irish sweetheart. After six months of hard work with Dr. Serbin, I no longer cried myself to sleep thinking of her. I'd even gotten to the point where I no longer fantasized about stabbing her with a butcher knife, then raping the shit out of her while she begged for forgiveness. But God damn it, I thought as I shook the last few lingering drops from my flaccid banana, at least I've got those TRO's off my back. And Serbin can stick it up his ass.

I re-entered the rectangular room with the Christmas tree lights. Without a word, I drank an entire pitcher of beer in two swallows, a total of nineteen seconds flat. Before anyone had a chance, I scrambled out the swinging door into the grey night. I heard the opening bar of "Help" as I headed down Polk Street. Every single time I've heard that tune I've taken it as some message from God, a warning of things to come, a perfect description of my mashed-potato character. "But now I'm not so self assured" hits it right on the button even for a grown, mature man like me that day. I'd heard it for the first time just two weeks before June MacAdoo kicked me out of her pad, and it was my theme song throughout the entire year that I became a television freak trying to get her out of my gut.

"I wonder if those creeps played it intentionally," I muttered as I staggered into the greyness of wet sidewalks and blinking lights along Polk Street. Young, blond fags with powder-blue eyes and soft shoes skipped along arm-in-arm. Chinese girls with long hair and black stockings carried metal pots into Ernie's Delicatessen for bean cake, barbequed duck, Chinese curds and steamed rice. Art students from the Art Institute, draftsmen from Heald's College and law students from S.F. Law School walked by in carefree abandon, none of them in pain, all with beautiful girls in red slippers. They had leather, beads and books and pipes and scabs of hair on their interesting faces. Polk Street at night was always Christmas Eve for lonely men such as myself.

For the third time that day I heard "A Whiter Shade Of Pale" coming at me from a record shop as I hurried to Maryjane's pad above Mario's Liquor Store. I knew that Bertha, a young, voluptuous Armenian nurse was staying with her. Between the two of them, I knew they'd give me the proper sendoff.

Maryjane was made of cotton candy. She wore rings of emerald and ruby glass. She and Bertha had seen me through the worst of my blue television period, taking me to all the swingers' bars in the Montgomery Street district and holding to me tightly when men tried to take them away. We'd gotten drunk so many times that most of the crew at JJ's thought I was sleeping with both of them.

The truth of the matter was we *were* sleeping together. Stoned drunk, late at night we'd pass out in whoever's bed happened to be handy. It boosted the hell out of my ego, but it did absolutely nothing for my abandoned lily. We often spoke of living together; I as their protector and they as my maids; but the hangover on the following day always seemed to argue against it.

I loved both of them as sisters, perhaps cousins, because they hated anyone that hurt me. They could cuss better than I. And for the past year, they'd helped me out of my affliction for my departed Irish lass. "You stupid, fucking shit! How can you dare to think of that skinny tramp? I think she's got lesbian problems," they'd throw it in my face whenever they saw me limping, my head in my chest and my tongue just hanging. And thus I went to see them to say my farewell.

"Oski-wa-wa!" they chimed in tandem as I entered.

"Fucking cats!" I kicked my way through hundreds of the monsters. The pad was a refuge for every stray tom on the street. It was their mission in life to care for crazies like myself and every bastard tiger others wouldn't feed. Each had a name, a box of his own and a cheap glass collar. Since no one in his right mind would look after this zoo, the girls could never go out of town for a weekend. And when out on dates with drunken seamen or Montgomery Street lawyers, their favorite line was, "Got to go now, boys. We've got to feed our children." They were so good at the art of put-on, the idiots actually let it go at that.

I shoved a longtailed tom off the rocking chair in the corner. Maryjane glared at me. "Don't be so fucking mean, Oski!"

"Yes, we'll have none of that tomfoolery," the girl with the gargantuan breasts ordered.

"What? You want *me* to stand?"

"He was there first," Maryjane argued. She picked up the grey animal as a mother does a child who's just fallen. She stroked his back and purred, "There, there Babypuss. He didn't mean to hurt you." She stuck the cat's face in mine. "Now kiss the baby, Oski."

It was either that or have her pissed at me for the rest of the night, so I bussed the bastard quickly on his nose.

"Now say you're sorry, you dirty old man!"

"Oh, for Christ sake, Bertha," I protested.

Maryjane, the more sensible of the two stepped in. "He doesn't know how to talk to Babypuss anyway, Berth."

"Okay, okay . . . I'm sorry."

Bertha stared at me in disgust. "You phony shit. You didn't mean it."

Before I could answer Ted Casey came into the small room from out of the kitchen. He wore a full beard now, was dressed in a blue Italian silk suit and carried a bottle of champagne with a goblet for me.

"What are *you* doing here?" I asked.

He filled the glass to the brim and handed it to me. "Here, this'll fix you right up."

Maryjane remained surprisingly silent. She gave an embarrassed look toward Bertha who turned to put some records on the hi-fi.

"Ted stopped by to drop some things off," she said to me in what sounded like the words of a young girl. I simply nodded my head and drank the Lejon, best of the cheap champagnes.

"Whyn't you broads get some rags on so's we can get movin?" Ted said.

To my instant surprise, the two toughest women I'd ever known marched into the bedroom without so much as a whimper. In two years of running around together, I was the only man to my knowledge whose orders they at least tolerated. And even with me, I'd never known them to obey an order without a fight or at least a "fuck you!"

"Stopped by to look for you today," I said to him.

"Oh, yeh? What's your problem?" His cheeks were puffed now. He'd lost the leanness of his seaman days. His arms, legs and fingers were stubs attached to an enormous belly filled to maximum capacity. But his sharply cut Italian silk suit wouldn't permit any visible fatness.

"I just wondered how you'd been," I said carefully. It seemed obvious the three were going out. The last I'd heard of him was when Charlie Fisher told me he wanted to cut off my balls, so I fenced around until I could find out what the real situation was.

"You sure you went to look for me? You weren't looking for Alice?"

"Well, you know. I hadn't seen either of you for over a year now. . . . How you been? Still on the ships?"

He poured me another goblet and I drank it right down. It seemed weak after the whiskey. "Oh, I been getting along. Just trying to do my best."

"I thought you'd be a captain by now," I put it to him.

"I am. Haven't you heard?" He smiled his brown teeth at me.

"Last I heard was you were into heavy dope . . . that true?"

"Osc, you know everything I do is heavy. I ain't one of those slimy cunts you run around with."

"Then you're not on the boats anymore? Is that what you're saying?"

"You gotta fend for yourself. I've been telling you, no one's gonna plant your potato patch. Gotta do it for yourself."

He poured more champagne and I drank it. He went to the hi-fi and looked through the batch for the right record. He always wanted his sessions to be just perfect. When he couldn't find what he wanted, he said, "Shit. No class." He took a small, single 45 from a shopping bag and put it on.

In his raspy, high, cutting voice he said, "Whyn't you just relax and zero in on this one? I hear you quit your job and fired your shrink today."

"How in the fuck do you know?" I shouted at him.

But before it could develop, they came at me again for the fourth time that day, that day of my rebellion, that first day of the seventh month of my thirty-third year . . . seven tall, thin, black-robed bishops. Seven crows in a row ascending deep, red velvet steps. With the Lejon deteriorating my rotting squash, four pink-eyed altar boys carried golden goblets in their precious, silver-tipped fingers, up the steps to the altar on ballerina tiptoes without spilling a drop of lamb's blood ". . . I was feeling kind of seasick with a whiter shade of pale."

"Ever tried mescalin?" Ted Casey calls to me from the deep.

I can't answer him. I'm an innocent, brown-eyed child of the sun. Just a peach-picker's boy from the West Side. Riverbank. My father's a janitor with only a third-grade education and my mother makes tortillas at 5:00 A.M. before she goes to the cannery.

"That sounds pretty groovy to me," Ted Casey intones.

"Yeh, what's wrong with that?" An Armenian girl with almond eyes oozes olive oil out of emerald lips.

A tall, thin gypsy in black patent boots spikes at the hard wooden floor. I used to call her Midge Magoda before she died of an overdose of cocaine. "I think he tried acid one time," Maryjane says to us.

I look at Ted Casey standing over me, and he becomes the dark bird of night out for a field mouse, a chicken or a little white baby lost in the woods. "Did anyone ever tell you you looked like an owl?" I say to him.

"I *am* The Owl." He fondles tangled, tiny snakes squirming from his otherwise insignificant chin.

Maryjane opens herself, her eyes wide, guilty, frightened. "Jesus, Ted what did you do to him?"

"There's nothing wrong with him. I only put three caps in the bottle," the Owl says.

"But he isn't used to it like you are," the gypsy says.

"Oh, don't worry, Maryjane," Bertha says. "I feel a little smashed myself."

"But he nearly drank the whole bottle," Maryjane says.

"He musta been thirsty," the Owl says.

"You really are an owl, you know?" I say to the man in the blue sailor suit from Italy. "And just today I was afraid of bloody noses when my secretary died."

"Come on, Oski, don't talk that way!" Maryjane orders me.

"Well, she did."

"Is that why you quit your job?" the man says to me.

"No, that's why I fired my psychiatrist," I say.

"Did you *really*?" Bertha speaks from out of a black cape. "You really socked it to him?"

"I just kicked him out of my shower . . . he wouldn't let me screw my friend's wife in peace," I babble on.

"Yes, that seems to be one of your hangups, my boy," Ted Casey says.

"Oski doesn't hurt anyone," Maryjane says.

"Just himself," Bertha looks down on me. I begin to fade into the orange rugs as the foghorns call out for more.

"My shrink says it's a form of self-love," I tell them.

"Jesus, Ted or Owl or whatever you call yourself . . . I'm worried." Maryjane comes to my rescue. "Do you think he'll be alright?"

The black owl rises and flutters his wings over my face. His pudgy body disappears. Two huge, round eyes penetrate into my entire being and consume the universe. Dark, deep green covers the earth on this last day of atonement.

The sound of the wailing organ stops. He slaps me sharply. A branch breaks the stillness of the green mist.

"Come out of it, man!"

Again he slaps my face. This time I feel the bone.

"Hey, motherfucker!" I shout at the fat Irishman from Brooklyn.

"He's all right," he says. "Come on, man. We got places to go. Wake up, daddy-o."

I jump up and notice that the three of them are staring anxiously.

55

I give one of my suave giggles. "What's wrong with you guys?"

"Oh, you big phony!" Bertha says.

Maryjane shakes her head and throws a right to my midsection. "You nasty, old man. What happened?"

I stretch and struggle to regain my composure. After all, Casey has not forgotten about my dirty habits. "Nothing. I just grabbed a little shut-eye while you guys got ready. Too much booze. I guess."

"But you can handle it, right?" Casey asks.

I give them my Bogart grin. "Shit, I can handle anything. Even your fucking drugs."

He nods his curly head and shows us his stained teeth. "Then let us go, hombre. You been out for an hour."

"You've never tried mescalin, have you Oski-wa-wa?" Maryjane asks.

"But Maryjane, Oscar here is a *lawyer*," Casey mocks.

"Not anymore he isn't," Bertha says.

"Well, I don't think it's right for you to give him that stuff without telling him," Maryjane says, perturbed. She is dressed in the long suede skirt and padded brown coat of a flamenco dancer.

"Why not? He came to look for dope today, didn't you Osc?"

"How'd you know?" I ask.

"I saw you."

"When I knocked on your door?"

"What's it matter?"

"But you didn't know what I wanted."

"Sure I did. . . . Like the man said, I'm into dope now. Lots of people come around to look for magic."

"Why didn't you open, then?" I asked.

"What, I got to open the door to every spic that knocks anytime he wants to cut my balls?"

Bertha cuts in, "Well, come on fellas. Are we ready? Or are we ready?"

Casey grabs her by the waist and swings her around. "We is ready, fat Bertha. We is ready."

"So they really call you Owl now?" I say to Casey.

"That's right, partner. I'm Owl. I'm *the* Owl now."

I stick my index finger into his breast pocket and say, "Well, Mr. Owl, in case they didn't tell you yet, I'm the Brown Buffalo."

"I know, I know you, hombre. And you can take anything, right? Mr. Macho."

Bertha removes his hand from around her waist. She throws her deliciously zoftig breasts into me. "My Brown Buffalo can take even Bertha Babes whenever he's ready too."

Because she comes to my defense and because I love her gorgeous cans against my chest I stick my tongue in her ear as a reward.

"Let's go to the Fior d'Italia," he says. "We'll come back and play that new record again."

"What record?" Maryjane asks.

"The one that freaked him."

With that, the four of us drive out into the night in the Owl's gigantic black Cadillac to North Beach in search of culture and cuisine from the Mafia.

Chapter Five

We roll gently in our black submarine down Bay Street past staid Victorian houses with nooks and crannies, Austrian shades and garages, lit to look like European brothels. We circle the two giant steeples above Peter and Paul's across from Washington Square where the old Italian men smoke stubby Toscanas and spit brown on the lawn, flaying their arms as they talk in operatic gestures; where young boys in short pants kick soccer while their fat mothers eat spumoni ice-cream with maybe another bambino already on the way. Grant Avenue is a block away. Here the yellow horde is cut off. From chow mein to pizza pies in one block. From slant-eyed, yellow people to black-eyed olive-oils all spliced by a single stop light at Grant & Broadway.

We don't wait for the nod from the parking lot attendant. The Owl merely stops the black machine, leaves the motor running and nods to the guard in front of the restaurant where Mr. Louis Scaglione has eaten twice daily in his pin-striped suit for fifty-four years.

"How they hanging, Hank?" the Owl says to the man in the long, red coat. The doorman salutes him with a tip of the cap and takes each woman by the hand. I follow behind them. My eyes are giant floodlights, concentric circles of white and red.

"This is real class, Owl," Maryjane, the gypsy says to him.

"Just another joint," he shrugs.

I tip-toe into another world of fat-red carpets, violet tablecloths, dazzling chandeliers, white camellias, red roses and purple spider-mums. Young olive trees and casual green elephant ears are potted along the sides. There are pink brick walls to separate the parties and in the center of the dining room is a fountain spouting yellow water from the pelvic bone of a whale. I see huge men in black suits and black glasses; old women with powder blue, short hair; young women with shivering gowns; furs of dead animals, diamonds from the caves of deepest Africa, rubies from the eyes of Asian dieties. Soft yellow lights, simple music from Mantovani, big black cigars, champagne, truffles, crepes suzettes, squab, wild rice, sweet-breads, saltimbocca, mushrooms and scampi alla casalinga . . . yes, sir, just another joint. Your Wing Lee's in the sky. Just like Trader JJ's!

A gorilla approaches the Owl. A giant of a man with manicured nails, a fistful of flesh and a mouth full of white teeth. Now they'll find me out. I know this can't last forever. My cheap Arrow shirt from Bond's—the only store that ever gave me credit in my life—the wide-collared job still has puke on it. My pockets are empty. They don't pay us until the fifteenth and I've never saved a penny in my life. Credit cards are not for the likes of a small town kid from Riverbank. Too bad I threw away my Bar license, I think to myself. Perhaps I could have used it for a credit card.

"Mr. Owl," the seven-foot tall gorilla says softly.

"Top'a the mornin, Hewey," the Owl says with a shine.

The gorilla grins. He hands Ted Casey two cigars. Ted takes a small package from inside his Italian blue silk suit.

"Panama Red," he says to the gorilla.

"Ah, yes. Good for the digestion." He pats his huge stomach.

"Or whatever," the Owl says. "You remember the Brown Buffalo here."

While the giant ape crushes my hand, I realize it's Hewey, the title holder in Ireland, the seaman Mary had picked up at Pier 23 the day I first met Ted Casey. The blood warms and lights up the arm. My breath escapes me. I can only nod a phony smile. Oh, yeh, we're old friends. I never dreamt of *your* broad. I never even thought of her, buddy.

"Nice to see you again, Hewey."

"Mr. Buffalo. How goes the law?"

"Justice everywhere," I say.

Ted says, "How are the hamburgers tonight, Hewey?"

"I suggest you try the pork and beans," he says with a straight face.

The women say nothing. They only have eyes for the diamonds and the furs. Hewey sits us next to the whale bone.

"Listen, whyn't you just tell Enrique the Owl is here with three special friends. We'll go the full boat." His voice drops. He is a banker now. A businessman.

"And? . . ."

"B.V. . . . uh, '52 will do just fine."

"At your service, my boy."

"And listen, Hewey . . . if you're nice, and you got the time . . . come and snort a little when you get the chance. I got me some super dope here. Blow your head right off."

We begin the feast amid hushed sounds of joy while the bald-headed waiter uses giant wooden forks to bale the alfalfa in front of our very eyes. With a manicured little finger pointing to the sky, he sprinkles out some integrated ants and before long we are scooping up beef tenderloin calabrese. I suck on the strips of filet cut with German steel and let the olive oil, the onions and the hot peppers fondle my aching tongue.

Bertha shows me her flaming nostrils. Maryjane vibrates her black eyes and together we salivate the baccala and ceci of the Cosa Nostra because it's Friday and each of us once made our Holy Communion. Ted Casey and the Owl trade seats, up and down, on and off, the musical chair routine of a promoter, an impresario who's brought his friends to wine with the upper classes, the culture vultures and the Mafiosi. I know that soon he'll take the contract from his briefcase, explain the terms and wait for me to sign up for the Fior d'Italia goon squad.

In the meantime I'm enjoying the last supper. And while the three of us play the eating scene from *Tom Jones*, the Owl snorts cocaine from a silver spoon, the tiny silver spoon that dangles from a chain about his fat neck. Occasionally Hewey and other gorillas come and pay homage to their master and take a whiff of the white powder.

"So you're all washed up with the legal trip, that it?" the Owl asks.

"He just needs a good vacation," the gypsy speaks.

My face is inside the cherries jubilee. The spoon is a shovel

61

in my hand.

"I'm in perfect health. If I can just stop my nose bleeding."

The Armenian hussy snaps at them. "Oh, shit why don't you guys just let him do what he wants?"

The green glow of brandy fire lights up the Owl's green eyes. He stabs the six dollar dessert, the luscious crepes suzettes and stuffs it in his beak. "Hey, cunt," he growls through the syrup, "you just powder your nose with some of this coke."

"Yeh, give me more of that snow," I demand. I take my Kaabar pocket knife, my own personal coke dispenser, scoop up a tipful of the white devil and suck in giant nostrils of slow, white heat through the tender veins of my Indian nose.

"Listen, you frog," Maryjane says to Ted Casey, "you can't talk to me that way!"

"Oh, let him get his rocks off," the Armenian shouts. "He thinks he's hot shit just 'cause these Mafia baddies kiss his ass."

"Mafia?" the Owl says. "You call this Mafia? Better'n those losers you travel with."

"Now just a minute, Ted Casey," Maryjane says. "You might be some big, hot turd around here . . ."

"Hey!" the Owl yells. "So how come you people are on my case? I was just trying to help the lad here."

"Exactly. Absolutely correct. I definitely need help. Give me more of that powdered mayonnaise."

We each take another turn. My nose itches. Gallons of green snot pour from my flat nose. I squint and perk and snort the stuff back into my bloodstream.

"Are you really Mediterranean?" I ask the Owl.

"Osc, old boy, I been telling you, I'm the god of the morning and the master of the evening star. What more can I tell you?"

"And I'm his fairy godmother," Bertha says.

"Hey, Bertha Babes, why don't you do your little thing for us?"

Maryjane claps her rings. "Yeh, come on Bad Girl!"

Ted Casey tenses. His nervous green eyes come to a squint. He says to me, "What she gonna do?"

"Just put on a little show for the gents here."

"But we got a show going, Buffalo. No need no more."

Maryjane shoots it to him. "What? Is the Owl a chicken?"

"The Owl *eats* chickens," I say as my eyeballs fall into my cognac.

The Armenian nurse rises with a flare. She drapes her fleshy arm around the neck of the chicken plucker. "Now I'm going to show you something new, Mr. Hot Stuff."

Bertha Bad Girl, she of the voluptuous knockers, spills her flesh over the crest of the red mini-dress and bumps her butt in a "Let Me Entertain You" routine. Her ruby red lips pouted like Miss Sally Rand, she throws out firm arms to the gaping waiters and kicks her solid legs at the dark-coated men with black glasses. "Let me show you how," the hussy whips it out. Maryjane and I whoop it up, we shout her on while Ted Casey shrivels into his hard silk suit. He squints side glances at Hewey, who stands near the elephant ear watching the patrons. No one budges as she thumps it out. At the last note she turns a full circle, points her beautifully round ass at us, lifts the mini and holds it long enough for us to applaud her tight silken panties printed with red candied apples. The remaining guests, the waiters and the three of us shout and stamp our feet.

I yell too loud, the blood rushes to my ancient head. My nostrils are aflame, my neck is burning. Why in God's name didn't I ever fuck her? I've seen those candied panties many times, but I never did more than swat her in the butt. And to top it off, June MacAdoo was jealous of her! I lost my Frisco broad for a dame I never even dry-fucked when I had the chance.

By the time Bertha reaches us the shouting is over. I am stretched across the purple table. The Owl holds a golden sword in both his hands and carves a hole in my enormous chest.

"What the shit are you doing to him?" Bertha yells. The Owl ignores her and takes a small dishful of mayonnaise which I'd ordered to throw over my tossed salad. Casey flinched when I asked Hewey if they had any hot sauce. "You know, the one in those little fifteen cent bottles. *Luisiana* hot sauce, if you got it." I said to the gorrilla.

The Owl fills the hole with mayonnaise. Then he carefully sprinkles a little white powder over the wound. When he finishes, he says to Bertha, "We're just making him feel better. He's had a hard day."

Maryjane reaches over and begins to stuff raspberry sherbet into the yellow lard under my belly button. "It's faster this way," she says.

"Oh, why didn't you tell me?" the Armenian nurse says. She takes my huge brown head ready for mounting and holds it in her arms like the Madonna. She puts her mouth full of emerald lips over my nose. She sucks on it, to save my life. My green snot puffs her face and fills it up like a carnival balloon. With her eyes against mine, she sucks and sucks until finally my head collapses like a rubber ball stuck with a dart. My shrivelled face is thrown

63

among the stale stogies on the floor. Black boots kick at me and the blood pours red carpets. I am under the ceiling that Procol Harum danced on and I see the underskirts of an apple orchard as someone rolls me across the floor of the Red Sea. And just when I think it will all come crashing upon me, smashing me to powder, just then I close my eyes and gently slide into the smooth, plush riding hearse of Casey's giant black submarine.

"He'll be all right," Casey says.

My face is pressed against the big, soft breasts of Bertha Bad Girl. I am in the back seat with her. The very first time I kissed a girl in high school we were riding in the back seat of Tommy Sawyer's '49 Chevy. We'd just finished dance band rehearsal. Tommy had Sheila Wright in the front and I had Madeline Hart in the back. When the car went around a curve I blacked out. I passed out completely. When I regained consciousness my mouth and my tongue were inside Madeline's saxophone lips. We necked for an hour until Tommy had to go home. I ended up walking home that night: five black miles of cow pastures, peach orchards and the voice of the second alto saxophone player saying to me, "You kiss like a horse."

The next day I got embarrassed as hell when my ma caught me kissing the palm of my right hand. She told my brother. Later when he asked me, I said I was just practicing for the next time.

"Do you think I kiss like a horse?" I ask Bertha with her tit in my mouth.

"Oski-wa-wa, you never told me!" she swoons. She presses my head tightly to her fleshy chest. My pants are on fire.

We are alone. The others have gone inside. We are parked next to the Volkswagen garage in front of Trader JJ's. The plush velvet of the black Cadillac fades into my skin. My peasant hands are searching the field for brown mice buried in between fleshy thighs. She gasps for air like a farmer's daughter lugging buckets of milk. It encourages me. I am atingle for the first time in over a year! I've not had my hand up a woman's dress since my Frisco broad kicked me out of her pad. I always told them, "It's those fucking pills my shrink makes me take. I just can't get it up."

"Christ, Bertha . . . I've just got to do it!"

"Well . . . what the fuck you waiting for?"

I am trembling. I never learned how to undress a broad without fucking it up. No one ever taught me the mechanics of snaps and buttons. My pants are ripping wide open. "Can't you take off that God damn cape?" I shout at her.

"Christ!" She is totally pissed.

"Come on. Give me a hand," I beg her.

She twists and turns and grunts and groans and removes all her clothes. I am practically in shock. I can't wait. My hands can't stop clawing at the delicacies of human flesh. And when she sees I am incompetent to even pull down my own zipper, she says, "Now, Oski . . . I'm going to really show you how."

She takes off my entire wardrobe without missing a stroke. All the while we pulsate in the dark of the Cadillac. To the rolling of thunder and lightning over San Francisco Bay. I am thundering across brown plains, the entire herd of frantic, brown buffalos are at my rear. I explode upon contact. When it slides into the tightness, before I can even give her a chance, the blasted beast goes off like a rocket in the deep.

"It doesn't matter," she says. "At least you had fun. That's enough for me this time."

"Next time will be better," I say as my eyes close and I relax my entire body for the first time in over a year. Sometime later I hear the door slam and I am alone. But it doesn't matter. The sleep feels good and warm. I finally got a piece of ass. I should fire my shrink more often. Or take more of the Owl's drugs, I seem to hear him say.

When I open my eyes, I am on my private stool next to the black safe in the corner. I see broken bits of stained glass and amoebas shivering through maple syrup. Sal is shouting at me.

"Come on! What do you want?"

Charlie, my fat artist friend slowly pulls on his pipe and says to Ted Casey, "What did you people do to him? I've never seen old Osc like this."

Bertha rips away at bristled hair over her cavernous eyes. "He ate too much. That's all."

Rinzberg, the balding cabbie who writes poetry for himself, is slobbering drunk, his white, pasty hands grab at her cans. Bertha doesn't pay any attention to him.

"Give me something green," I say to Sal, the black Sicilian.

"Nothing doing!" he barks. "Not till someone pays for the last round."

"I didn't order any fucking round," I shout.

"You drank it."

"Here, Foti, I got it," Casey says, shoving a crisp fifty dollar bill at him.

"Ain't you got something smaller, hotshot?"

"Can't handle it?"

I let the green Chartreuse slide down my tongue. When Sal gives Casey the change, he leans over and trys to whisper, "Listen, pal, you better keep your eye on him. Looks to me like he's having a hard time."

"Ah, the Brown Buffalo can take it," Casey says.

"Yeh, I know. But I hear he's going to be traveling tomorrow."

Suddenly, the Armenian dairy queen throws up her hands. "Oh, shit, Rinzberg! Let's dance. Then you can feel all you want."

The cabbie with the bulging jowls has his tongue hanging out. He looks toward me and curls his thin lips. "You gargantuan, gorgeous hunk of woman. Come to me, I'll show you how it feels to be with a man that can," he says for my benefit.

I grab his arm tightly. "Hey, Rinzberg."

He tries to shake me off. "Get your filthy paws off me!"

I lean over and whisper to him, "No, listen . . . Do you remember calling MacAdoo late one Sunday night?"

He pulls and shrugs. "I don't want to talk about your skinny bitch."

I hold his flabby arm in a vise. "You remember, you fuck. You called her real late and tried to hit her up for a date when I was living with her."

"Ah, fuck, man. That was over a year ago."

"I know . . . I just wanted you to know . . . I was flat on my back, in her bed while she talked to you and listened to your romantic slobbering."

"So what?"

"I just wanted you to know . . . I had my hand in her pussy when she turned you down, you cheap hack."

"And you've been waiting all this time to tell me?" he laughs at me.

Bertha has been watching the dancers. "Rinzberg! Do you want me or not?"

Hot Gin John, the big, grey haired engineer whose eyes sparkle and bulge when he hovers over a woman, is leaning against the juke box for support. He's had ten glasses of warm gin with a pinch of lemon, and the original dirty old man is scouting the floor for a score. He desperately pulls at his zipper in time with the music.

It is all madness, I think to myself. Five years of madness in this hideout. No wonder I'm cracking up. I take the green death into my hands and see my reflection in waves on the mirror behind the bar. I am the son of Lorca, I remind myself. The only poet of this century worth reading. Did he suffer with those black eyes?

That smooth, long greaser hair; did it make him hurt?

Who are these strange people, these foreigners that don't understand me? Friends all, yet they bring me memories of pain and long-suffering. I definitely must run. I've got to go hide, to seek my fortune in the desert, in the mountains, Anywhere but here.

Even that brief jab with Bertha, of what value was that? Now she bumps and grinds with Rinzberg, a baldheaded bastard who'd steal your woman from under your eyes if you let him. I arise and stagger between the dancers. I go into the phone booth. Jose told me June was still living in the same place. Going with some fucking accountant from Macy's now. I dial her number. What'll I say? Surely she'll remember me, won't she?

I hear the nasal voice of my beloved. "Hello?"

"Hi . . . it's me." I say. My heart thumps away, my head spins. I am alone in this green phone booth next to the toilet.

She hesitates. "Uh . . ."

"Oscar," Jesus, maybe I should hang up.

"Oscar? . . . I thought you'd gone."

In my eye I can see the short pageboy brown hair. "No, I'm still here."

"Jose told me you were splitting town."

"This joint's just full of big mouths."

There is silence for a moment. "I was hoping I'd see you."

My stomach gives in. What? Did I hear right? "Really?"

"It's been over a year, you know."

Sure enough, sweetie. Tonight is my night, I think. "Well, are you busy tonight?"

"Sort of . . . I've got company."

Down, down, down. My heart stops. Emptiness in this crowded green booth. "I'm leaving in the morning," I say faintly.

"Could you stop by before you split?"

What's this? You mean she doesn't have someone playing with her snatch while I hustle her? "Are you inviting me?"

"It's been over a year, Oscar."

What a fool, I think. Why must I always be negative? She didn't say it was a man, did she? I'll try once more. "Uh, what do you suggest?"

"Well, look . . . I'm getting married."

"And you want to see me? What the hell for?" I shout.

"Well . . . to say hello . . ."

What in the fuck is this? "You want my approval?"

"Come on, dear. Don't be mean to me."

"Well, I don't approve. You'll have to do it without me."

"All right, don't get your ulcers in a state."

"For Christ sake, June, what do you *want* with me?" I am desperate.

"Look, honey . . . can you pay me back the money I lent you?"

"What? That's why you want to see me?"

"And to say . . . goodbye."

"Fuck . . . goodbye!"

I slam it hard. I don't even bother to see if my dime came back. I return to the bar, my teeth grinding. I sit and put a cigarette to my mouth, look for a match. A tall, balding stranger is sitting next to me. In the mirror I can see him giving me the once over. He smiles sweetly from the corner of his eyes. He whips out a Zippo and fires me up. I simply nod, for I have already noticed the short distance between his right and left eyes. It is my secret way of detecting fags. I know he will speak.

And the first thing the idiot says is, "Are you by any chance Samoan?"

All my life strangers have been interested in my ancestry. There is something about my bearing that cries out for history. I've been mistaken for American Indian, Spanish, Filipino, Hawaiian, Samoan and Arabian. No one has ever asked me if I'm a spic or a greaser. Am I Samoan?

"Aren't we all?" I groan.

He reached his hand toward me. "You don't mind my asking, do you?"

"Of course not," I say calmly as I reverse the lit end of the cigarette so that the flame is cupped in the palm. I reach for his handshake.

He screams like a woman in distress with her skirt held high. I puff my meanness as he licks at the burn and whimpers, "You sonofagun. You've burned the dickens out of my hand."

"I know."

"But why? I didn't do anything. I don't even know you."

"I guess it's my Samoan blood."

Sal rushes to my defense. He points his finger at the fag. "Out!"

"But I didn't do anything."

"Out, out!" he shouts, his hands stiffly on the bar.

The old fag picks himself up and begins to drag himself out.

"Next time don't bother people you don't know," Sal piles it on as the fag walks out. My father turns to me and says, "What do you want to pick on people like him for?"

Suddenly we hear a scream. There is shouting and running.

A pitcher of beer is on the floor. Maryjane screams, "Jose!"

I turn and see the Mexican Mystic in all his glory. He's come out of the toilet carrying his Big Mac coveralls in his hands. He has long white legs and wears thick, woolen, white athletic socks. Except for my cousin Manuel, I have never seen such a long cock.

"Get a load of that, will you," Maria screeches.

The great artist takes his prick in his hand and points it toward her. "Don't you just wish you had this?"

By this time Sal is around the bar. While some dance and others scream, Sal takes Jose by the back of his railroad shirt and pushes him to the swinging doors. Jose goes without a word. Sal kicks him in the ass out into the dark. Everyone yells and claps and stomps their feet.

"Jesus, what's going on here tonight?" Sal shouts.

"Let's roll again," Ted Casey says.

"Yeh, let's gamble," I say.

"With what? You ain't got no loot," Sal pushes me.

"I'll roll for anything, anytime," I yell at him.

He picks up the dice cup. "Okay, hotshot. Just don't tell me to put in on the tab."

"Stiffereeno," I say. And then I lower my voice, "By the way, did Don tell you?"

"Tell me what?" the black Sicilian asks.

Casey rolls a full house: three fives and two sixes.

"I need some money."

I roll four fours. Win.

Casey says, "What do you need money for?"

"I got to hit the road."

"Running ain't gonna help you," he instructs me.

"You want to be my father, too?"

The Owl says, "No, no. You got me all wrong. I hire out as a guru for people like you."

"You? A guru?" I laugh.

"Why not?" the Owl says. "Don't take much to learn how to om."

"Fuck. You're just a dope peddler."

We roll again. Casey leans over and whispers in my ear. "Listen, fat man. If you get stuck somewhere, just send me a smoke signal. I've got better magic than anything you'll find on the road."

We roll and roll and drink until my head is bursting. The last thing I remember saying to Sal is, "I need a couple of hundred."

I don't remember when or how, but he must have given it to me since the next day I had over $200 in my pocket. My memory is etched with one final scene: the doors suddenly crash open. There is the huge roar of a space ship swooping in with the wind roaring at the back of John Tibeau, the self-proclaimed poet of Trader's, wearing a full-length white cast on his left leg and riding the back of a monstrous black Harley Davidson. Sal dashes around the bar, and the young Irish lad from Chicago circles the dance floor, one foot ahead of the old man chasing him with a three foot long axe handle that he keeps behind the bar just for such occasions.

The black-haired poet speeds out, showering the bar with carbon and sparks. Sal stands at the door with the handle over his head.

"You crazy sonofabitch. I'll kill you if you ever come back."

My face falls into my glass. The iceberg freezes my nose. I am numb. In a trance, a stupor. Passed out. Death is welcome after the events of this day, the first of July, 1967.

Chapter Six

With thundering hoofbeats hammering and kicking whirlwinds of dust to my rear, I eat up the burning sands and concentrate on the white line, my only guide. Sacramento, Lake Tahoe and Shell stations. I pass up long-haired hitchhikers. I discard empty Budweisers along the trail just in case I lose my direction now that I am without my shrink, my guru and their magic. Tall buildings and rectangular slabs of pavement sink behind me as I dig my claws into the gas pedal of my green '65 Plymouth. With a head full of speed, a wilted penis and a can in my hand, my knuckles redden as I hold tightly to the wheel and plunge headlong over the mountains and into the desert in search of my past . . .

Although I was born in El Paso, Texas, I am actually a small town kid. A hick from the sticks, a Mexican boy from the other side of the tracks. I grew up in Riverbank, California; post office box 303; population 3,969. It's the only town in the entire state whose essential numbers have remained unchanged. The sign that welcomes you as you round the curve coming in from Modesto says, "The City Of Action."

Manuel Mercado Acosta is an *indio* from the mountains of Durango. His father operated a mescal distillery before the revolutionaries drove him out. He met my mother while riding a motorcycle in El Paso.

Juana Fierro Acosta is my mother. She could have been a singer in a Juarez cantina but instead decided to be Manuel's wife because he had a slick mustache, a fast bike and promised to take her out of the slums across from the Rio Grande. She had only one demand in return for the two sons and three daughters she would bear him: "No handouts. No relief. I never want to be on welfare."

I doubt he really promised her anything in a very loud, clear voice. My father was a horsetrader even though he got rid of both the mustache and the bike when FDR drafted him, a wetback, into the U.S. Navy on June 22, 1943. He tried to get into the Marines, but when they found out he was a good swimmer and a non-citizen they put him in a sailor suit and made him drive a barge in Okinawa.

We lived in a two-room shack without a floor. We had to pump our water and use kerosene if we wanted to read at night. But we never went hungry. My old man always bought the pinto beans and the white flour for the tortillas in 100-pound sacks which my mother used to make dresses, sheets and curtains. We had two acres of land which we planted every year with corn, tomatoes and yellow chiles for the hot sauce. Even before my father woke us, my old ma was busy at work making the tortillas at 5:00 A.M. while he chopped the logs we'd hauled up from the river on the weekends.

Reveille was at 6:00 A.M. sharp for me and my older brother, Bob. Radio Station KTRB came on the air each morning with "The Star Spangled Banner." A shrill, foggy whistle woke us to the odors of crackling wood in the cast iron stove cooking the perfectly rounded, soft, warm tortillas.

"All right, boys. Up and at 'em," the wiry *indio* calls out to me and Bob. Sleep is for the lazy, those whom my parents detest, the slow-minded types afraid of the sunlight. And so to prove my worth I'm always the first one to jump up, stand on the bed and place my hand respectfully over my heart—I'm only a civilian—to show my allegiance to my father's madness for a country that has given him a barge and a badge at Okinawa in exchange for an honorable discharge. And made him a citizen of the United States of America to boot.

72

After the salute we scramble to dress while on KTRB one of the Maddox brothers says to Rose, "Give us a great big smile, Rose." She giggles and they stomp away to an Okie beat. Roll call comes on the Acosta ship at exactly 6:10 on the button. My father waits for his crew outside. We stand in line, my brother, myself and my mother who is trying to lose weight.

She has been on a diet all my life. She has a definite concern about people being overweight. She has nagged me and my sisters— my brother Bob was always skinny—until we all ended up with some doctor or another; but I stayed fat and she has always had a fine body, even sexy you might say.

After we eat our scrambled eggs and chorizo guzzled down with Mexican chocolate, we trudged through the well-worn paths across empty lots with wild wheat to Riverbank Grammar School where I learned my p's and q's from Miss Anderson. At noon we ran down Patterson Road for lunch. Two miles in fifteen minutes flat. My mother was of the strict opinion that you cannot learn without a hot lunch in your stomach. So we were permitted exactly thirty minutes to finish up our daily fights at the old black oak tree. A tree with gnarled branches with small, cork-like, burnt balls we used for floaters when we waited for catfish down at the river near the Catholic church where the sisters taught us about sin and social politics.

Bob and I had to chop wood for the evening meal. We had to pump the water into tin tubs for our nightly bath. And unless we bathed and washed the dishes, we couldn't turn on the little brown radio to listen to *The Whistler, The Shadow,* or *The Saturday Night Hit Parade* with Andy Russell, the only Mexican I ever heard on the radio as a kid. We would sit and listen while we shined our shoes. During the commercials my mother would sing beautiful Mexican songs, which I then thought were corny, while she dried the dishes. "When you grow up, you'll like this music too," my ma always prophesied. In the summer of '67, as a buffalo on the run, I still thought Mexican music was corny.

Usually, my old man would wait until we got in bed before he gave us our nightly lectures. Then he'd pull out a blue-covered book they'd given him in the Navy called *The Seabee's Manual.* It was the only book I ever saw him read. He used to say, "If you boys memorize this book, you'll be able to do anything you want." It showed you how to do things like tie fantastic knots, fix boilers on steam ships and survive without food and water when lost at sea. Admittedly, it helped when I took my entrance exams into Boy Scout Troop 42, but it didn't offer any advice on how to get rid of ulcers or the ants in my stomach. Its primary wisdom was its advice against waste. The horsetrader was so hung up on this principal sin that once he made me go to bed without supper because I'd filled a glass with water when I only required half the precious liquid.

"Why can't you fill it halfway? Then if you want more, fill it about one-fourth . . . etcetera," he'd tell us in total seriousness. To this day I get a twinge of guilt when I throw away water, leftovers and old clothes that I can't possibly use.

We used to go to the garbage dump down by the old aluminum plant, which to my knowledge never produced aluminum. Immediately after its construction Tojo and FDR got into it and the place was converted into a shell-casing plant. That event, along with the Riverbank Canning Company, placed Riverbank on the map. We had one of the three shell-casing plants in the country during the Second World War and the largest tomato paste cannery in the world.

We'd take a truckful of junk to the dump and spend the entire morning searching through the rotting, burning piles of trash, broken furniture, old clothes, busted tools and old family items, all of us in search of things that the horsetrader thought could still be saved under the rules of *The Seabee's Manual.* By the time we got done, the truck was as full as when we left. Then the singer and the *indio* would get into it. And when he'd turn his back to her, shake his head and say "You just don't understand," she'd start in on me and Bob. But she never contradicted him in our presence.

You'd better do what your dad tells you, *hijo*," she'd warn us. Even when she knew it was madness, when she suspected he was suffering from shell-shock, still she never disagreed with his instructions to his sons. She'd simply take another aspirin and sing Mexican songs, dreaming maybe of what might have been had she not become a captain's wife.

Even the time he gave us the ultimate lesson on becoming "a man," she didn't say a word. We were all at the supper table. I was wolfing down hot, fresh corn with huge glasses of milk. I'd eat so fast that even when I dropped a piece of meat on the adobe floor or spilled the Koolaid, I wouldn't miss a stroke. He warned me of the effect it would have on both my character and my stomach. Every single night of my childhood, my folks bugged me about my speed. It got to where I even tried eating with my left hand to slow me down, but after three weeks I became ambidextrous and it wouldn't work anymore. I consoled myself with the idea that even though it didn't help my diet any, it would still be of use in case I ever got my right hand chopped off by the Japs.

That night, my old man said, "If you can eat a spoonful of your mother's chili, I'll give you a penny."

I looked at my brother. He wasn't about to take up the challenge. He didn't pay as much attention to my dad as I did. For some reason, he wasn't that interested in becoming a man.

"Right away? A penny for every spoonful?" The six-year-old kid said.

"Don't you trust me?"

My brother merely laughed when he saw the tears running down my fat, brown cheeks after the third spoonful. But I proved my point. I never backed off from any challenge.

My mother just shook her head. She disapproved of his madness, she even tried to imagine there might be some mystery that she, as a mere woman, couldn't understand.

Frugality and competition were their lot. The truth of it was they both conspired to make men out of two innocent Mexican boys. It seemed that the sole purpose of childhood was to train boys how to be men. Not men of the future, but *now*. We had to get up early, run home from school, work on weekends, holidays and during vacations, all for the purpose of being men. We were supposed to talk like *un hombre*, walk like a man, act like a man and think like a man. When they called us from the corner lot to play keep-away, we couldn't go until we finished pulling weeds from the garden. And while the gang gathered behind the grocery store to smoke cigarette butts, we had to shine our shoes and read the *Seabee's Manual*. In fact the only times we could read funny books was when my father was in the Navy. Nothing would infuriate him more than to catch us browsing through *Captain Marvel* or *Plastic Man*. Men, after all, didn't waste their time reading funny books. Men, he'd tell us, took life seriously. Nothing could be learned from books that were funny.

I used to think that only my father was mad. I doubted that the fathers of my friends in the barrio taught them the same things. But one day I learned differently. Walking home from school on a Tuesday afternoon, I spit on the picture of an American flag. It was Victory Stamp Day. We used to save them the way some people collect green stamps.

We had been lectured by Miss Anderson on the art of self preservation in case of an enemy attack. Although she spoke strictly about the Japanese, I always pictured the real enemy as not only a Kamikaze with the red rising sun on his wings, but also some old man with an enormous fountain pen who sent printed letters to the poor families living in small towns. FDR was as much my enemy as were the Japs. After all, it was he, not Tojo, who drafted my old man. He's the one who made my mother and my brother cry for a whole month after we drove my dad down to the post office. He's the one who took a razor blade and cut out entire sentences from the little letters that looked like telegrams that my father wrote us from Okinawa, Iwo Jima and Tarawa. And when my father said *they* hadn't told him how much longer he'd have to drive the barge, we knew he referred to FDR not Tojo.

So you have eight rag-a-tag ten year-old brown-baked Mexican boys marching single file along the curb in front of the old PT&T. Oscar sees a leaflet with the picture of the American flag. He spits!

"Hey, look what Oscar did," Johnny Gomez tells the others. He stands back, points to the leaflet as if it were some snake. The others circle around and shake their heads.

"What'd you do that for?" his brother, David demands of me.

"Why not? It's just a picture," I explain.

"That's the American flag, stupid!"

"So what?"

"So don't do it no more."

"Why? You gonna make me?"

David beat the shit out of me. While I dusted my pants off and wiped the blood from my elbows, they all laughed at me.

"You ain't so tough," the short little Indian said to me.

"Oh, yeh?" He got on top of me and pinned my arms to the ground with his knees. I had to give up . . . but only to start again with Alfonso when he said I was a chicken. As things turned out, I had to fight each of them that afternoon. I lost every single fight.

The seven whipped my ass on that day that I spit on the picture of my father's flag. I have never, to this day, had any respect for that flag or that country. You can blame it on my childhood experiences. Politics has nothing to do with it. I have no ideology. I've been an outlaw out of practical necessity ever since. And I have never backed off from a fight.

My old man taught me to fight dirty. He said, "Don't start anything. But if you have to fight, don't fool around. Pick up a stick, a rock or anything that's hard. You hit them on the head a few times and they'll never pick on you again."

He bought us boxing gloves and a punching bag for Christmas. After a while, none of the guys in the neighborhood my age wanted to come over and work out. Years later, as a senior in high school, I won the heavyweight boxing championship by hitting Harry

Greene below the belt until he couldn't stand up. When his manager ran into the ring to protest, I punched him too. Some of his followers chased me into the locker rooms after they gave me the medal. I picked up a track shoe with spikes and held them at bay until my football coach, Joe Sigfried ordered them out.

Living in Riverbank was no different than living in a strange, foreign town. I was an outsider then as much as I am now. Particularly during the first three years, Bob and I had to defend ourselves against the meanest and toughest boys on the list because we were considered "easterners." They said we weren't *real* Mexicans because we wore long, black patent leather boots and short pants, which my mother bought for us in Juarez just before we boarded the Greyhound bus to join up with my father, who'd left the year before to seek the riches of California's golden peach orchards.

California, then, was a land of *Pochos*. These California Mexicans were not much higher than the Okies with whom they lived. They spoke English most of the time, while we looked upon life "out west" simply as a temporary respite from the Depression. The five bucks a week my old man earned as a mechanic in El Paso hadn't been quite enough to satisfy my mother's dreams. She wanted a sewing machine, a house with electricity and running water. She never dreamed of actually owning a house, she just wanted to live in one with all the modern conveniences she read about in the Sears & Roebuck catalogue. So, when we left *El Segundo Barrio* across the street from the international border, we didn't expect the Mexicans in California to act like gringos.

But they did. We were outsiders because of geography and outcasts because we didn't speak English and wore short pants. And so we had to fight every single day. Until the day Bob beat up Jimmy Pacheco, the youngest of a bunch of Apaches who lived in the edge of the barrio with ten brothers and about seven dogs. They were the only ones in the entire neighborhood that had a wire fence around their property. They were always slaughtering pigs and goats and young bulls, getting drunk on tequila and drinking raw blood with fresh onions. But one day Bob grabbed Jimmy by the wrist and flung him against the trunk of an old black oak tree and that was that. Jimmy didn't fool anyone with the long-sleeved shirts he wore for weeks after the incident. We all knew he had a cast underneath. Generally, the *Pochos* quit picking on us after that. Not that they accepted us as part of their tribe, but they simply quit fucking with us. I never had to fight a Mexican again until I joined the revolution some thirty years later.

The fight with Pacheco didn't end the war, however. Our

biggest battle-front opened at seven-thirty in the morning at the railroad tracks which marked the edge of Okie Town. At night and on weekends we fought the Mexicans in the neighborhood, but during the day and at school we had to fight off the Okies. We had an unspoken rule that you never fought one of your own kind in front of others. In the battle for group survival you simply don't weaken your defenses by getting involved in family squabbles in front of the real enemy.

We had to fight the Okies because we were Mexicans! It didn't matter to them that my brother and I were outcasts on our own turf. They'd have laughed if we'd told them that we were easterners. To them we were greasers, spics and niggers. If you lived on the West Side, across from the tracks, and had brown skin, you were a Mexican.

Riverbank is divided into three parts, and in my corner of the world there were only three kinds of people: Mexicans, Okies and Americans. Catholics, Holy Rollers and Protestants. Peach pickers, cannery workers and clerks.

We lived on the West Side, within smelling distance of the world's largest tomato paste cannery. With its hordes of flies and the ugly stench of rotting waste on hot, summer days, the West Side was tucked a safe distance from the center of town where the Americans lived. Every home had a garden, at least a rose bush or two and if nothing else, a couple of chickens. We grew vegetables not for victory, but for survival during the frosted, tully-fogged winter months after the peaches, walnuts, tomatoes, grapes and olives had been picked. And long before it became fashionable for the American women to plant flowers and lemon trees in cute little bonnets and white gloves, the Mexican women were watering their roses and chili plants on Saturday mornings while we went to our catechism classes at the Lady of Guadalupe.

The West Side is still enclosed by the Santa Fe Railroad tracks to the east, the Modesto-Oakdale Highway to the north and the irrigation canal to the south. Within that concentration only Mexicans were safe from the neighborhood dogs, who responded only to Spanish commands. Except for Bob Whitt and Emitt Brown, both friends of mine who could cuss in better Spanish than I, I never saw a white person walking the dirt roads of our neighborhood.

If you climb the water tower next to the railroad depot, you can see Okie Town to the east. Riverbank is flat, farming country. Except for the bank and the Masonic lodge, there are no three-story dwellings or structures for miles around. I always wanted to climb that aluminum colored, 10,000-gallon water storage tank, but Harry March, who owned the five and dime always warned against it. He looked like John L. Lewis and sold us cigarettes if we scribbled a note and pretended it was from our parents. I used to ask for Wings and sign my father's name, even though we both knew he was away in the Navy. "If they catch you, they'll put you in the hoosegow," he'd tell us when we stopped by on the way home from school for our afternoon ice-cream cone.

One day I couldn't wait anymore to do my part for the war effort Miss Anderson kept talking about. I wanted my father home because my mother was going crazy. She ate nothing but aspirins and oranges, drank black coffee and beat us with belts, rubber hoses, ice-hooks. Even though I'd sort of taken over the family at the age of ten, got to zip up my mother's dresses when she dressed for the cannery and had the final word on whether my sisters could go to the movies, still I wanted the sailor back home.

The headlines of the *Modesto Bee* made us cry every day, even when Mr. McClatchy said we'd pounded the daylights out of the Japs. The constant flow of mile-long troop trains with soldiers herded in like cattle was a daily reminder of my uselessness as a civilian. We'd go down to the railroad and wave at the brave men headed for San Francisco on their way to fight the Japs. They'd give us pennies and nickels and once in a while ask us to bring our sisters to say hello. Mine was practically still in diapers, so I couldn't offer much of that.

I have even taken to looking for the red cellophane strips from Lucky Strikes packs which Harry March had told us could be exchanged for German Shepherd seeing-eye dogs for the crippled veterans. After a year I only had 200 of them. I'd had enough arithmetic to know that at that rate I'd be picking up dirty, empty cigarette packs for five more years. We tried to save newspapers, but it didn't amount to much. And I knew it would take the rest of my life to save ten pounds of tin foil from Juicy Fruit and the insides of the cigarette packs.

So one day I finally made my decision to join the resistance. I climbed to the top of the lily tree in our back yard. This tree with the purple blossoms and little green balls the size of steelies— the best marble you can pick for playing Fish—this was my own personal, private place. Bob was the owner of the eucalyptus tree, and we all shared the fruits of the plum, the fig and the almond trees; but no one could climb my lily tree without my permission.

I carry my pump-action .22 strapped to my shoulder as I carefully and quietly climb the thirty-foot-tall sniper post. The enemy planes fly day and night over this land. I just have to wait. Gary Cooper didn't complain when he had to sit in that tree with the Japs marching underneath, the flies and gnats driving him crazy in that hot, steaming jungle, did he? . . . I hear the drone in the distance. I close my eyes. You can tell by the hum of the motor whose side he's on. And when it is overhead I take careful aim. I know it *looks* like a P-38, but that's a disguise . . . I shoot.

I wait for it to fall, but somehow it keeps flying towards the aluminum plant . . . I wipe the sweat from my brow and think it through again. What would Coop do in this situation? I have only one bullet left. One shot. Do I wait for another plane? Of course they heard the blast from my rifle. Soon they'll be here. I'm not afraid of the torture. I can take anything, remember? But a man has to destroy any target, any supply of war material, do anything that will hurt the Nips. It doesn't have to be a moving target. It doesn't have to be a human . . .

And there it sits, big as day. No more than one block from my scope is the infamous water tower. The whole town depends upon it. Cut off their water supply and you'll have them in the palm of your hand in a week. Does the Geneva Convention actually prohibit sniper action against the civilian population? What would Miss Anderson say about this? Fuck it! I've got to help my father get home any way that I can. After all, *this is war!* Surely God will understand even if the sisters don't. Look at Humphrey Bogart. He's still alive, isn't he? And how many has he snuffed out? I squeeze the trigger and close my eyes.

Two days later I take a casual stroll to the railroad depot. Just going down to say hello to the troops, I tell my ma. For two whole days and nights I've not even dared to look toward the east. It's bad luck to look for death and destruction. No one's mentioned it, but I've been certain all weekend that the entire population will soon be dying of thirst. The fact that our faucet keeps pumping clear water doesn't throw me; I know they're on the spare tank now. By tomorrow it'll be all over with.

Without looking up, I stand under the palm trees in the little park behind the Santa Fe Depot. When I'm certain no one is looking, I look up toward the water tank. I squint my eyes to see the damage. I look for evidence of a flood. Something. It's possible, of course they already dried it out, sucked the water up with some huge pump. Good soldiers always hide their true battle conditions. Besides, how can I really be sure? I haven't binoculars to be positive. I'll merely report it as an "attempt." I didn't do it for any God-damn purple heart anyway! The old man will simply have to take my word for it. He knows I never lie to him. He knows perfectly well I've never lied to him since that day he hung me from a rafter in the chicken coop.

We were pulling weeds from the tomatoes. My young uncle Hector started it all. He threw the first rock at Bob. My brother thought it was me and threw a clod the size of a pumpkin. The captain warned us twice. The third time he ordered us inside. Before he found a belt some Americans stopped by to purchase some corn. We sold it for fifty cents a dozen and an extra one in case you found one with worms. While the horsetrader picked the corn from the stalks, Hector talked us into stuffing newspapers under our V-8's. "Don't forget to pretend when he hits us," my uncle said. . . . Well, I blew it. I forgot. I should have rubbed onions in my eyes.

When the captain discovered the sport's pages of the *Modesto Bee* under my shorts, he asked, "Okay, you cheaters, whose idea was it?"

Shit, not even my old man can make me talk once I've made up my mind. I am loyal to the core. Even when he marched us to the chicken coop under the plum tree, did you see me cry? When he made the three of us stand on that four-by-four, tied the rope around our necks, did you hear me beg for mercy?

"When you're ready to talk, I'll cut you down," he said.

Even when he walked out, leaving us there to die I said nothing. Despite the fact I was the youngest of the three, you didn't see me holding up any white flag of surrender. Though as the blood curdled in my legs, even cramps of electrical shocks up my spine didn't do a thing. I knew my mother would find us with our tongues hanging out when she came for the eggs in the morning. And when that mean bantam rooster pecked at my feet, when we could no longer hear my father's voice outside, you still didn't hear me cry, did you?

It was Hector who chickened out and called for help. "Manuel, you better cut me down or I'll tell 'ama." Who knows how long the captain would have let us hang if Hector hadn't been his kid brother? Whatever influence or authority Hector had over me because he was my uncle and five years older, he lost it that afternoon in the chicken coop. And but for his lack of character, I'd probably have never started on those nasty habits in the shower.

During the summers we used to pick peaches. My father would challenge the three of us to a race. If Bob, Hector and me could pick more lugs of peaches than the captain, he'd buy us a watermelon and take us to the canal after work. We always lost because we took an hour for lunch while the old man kept picking away, but he took us to swim anyway. The sweltering heat and the itching peach fuzz didn't bother Indians like him. But laggards and sissies such as we were had to plunge and dip and show off in front of girls at the canal during the lunch hour to feel better.

If it hadn't been for my fatness I'd probably have been able to do those fancyassed jackknifes and swandives as well as the rest of you. But my mother had me convinced I was obese, ugly as a pig and without any redeeming qualities whatsoever. How then could I run around with just my jockey shorts? V-8's don't hide fat, you know. That's why I finally started wearing boxers. But by then it was too late. Everyone knew I had the smallest prick in the world. With the girls watching and giggling, the guys used to sing my private song to the tune of "Little Bo Peep" . . . "Oh, where, oh where can my little boy be? Oh, where, oh where can he be? He's so chubby, *panson*, that he can't move along. Oh, where, oh where can he be?"

I tried like hell to stop eating ice-cream and tortillas with mayonnaise, but I still always stayed five or ten pounds overweight. And no matter what I did or what I thought, even when I asked the Virgin Mary to make me a man and give me at least a bit of pubic hair, still my prick was an inch or two smaller than all the rest.

In fact, if it hadn't been for Vernon Knecht I might have remained the deformed freak that I was to this day. He was a big, red-headed German kid who taught me how to leave markings on trees and traffic arrows made of rocks when I studied for my merit badges with Troop 42. When I was twelve we went on a hiking and camping weekend with our fag Boy Scout leader out at the Oakdale Reservoir, and I was instructed to be Vernon's *buddy*. In case you drowned, got lost, or were attacked by Indians, you were supposed to have a buddy. Since Vernon was a First Class Scout and about three years older, the tenderfoot that I was leaned on his every word. So that night, under the pup tent while the summer rain kept us all inside, I asked him how to make the bugger grow.

"Shit, you mean you don't know how to jack off?"

"You mean pull it?" I asked my guide.

He whipped out his long, white dick and said, "Yeh, man. Push and pull . . . just like this."

When Hector, brother Bob and cousin Manuel used to make fun of my obesity and little penis, I would yell through my teeth, "At least I don't pull it." They always got a kick out of that and called me a liar. I had to show them the palms of both my hands to prove that I didn't masturbate.

"You see any warts?" I'd ask.

So that weekend at the Oakdale Reservoir, I told Vernon Knecht, "I don't want to do anything dirty. I haven't made my confirmation yet."

"What do you mean?" the German infidel asked.

"Shit, man, how would you confess that to a priest? . . . You think he'd believe me if I told him I did it to make it grow?"

"Well, fuck, man. Just don't tell him."

I lost most of my religion the same night I learned about sex from old Vernon. When I saw the white, foamy suds come from under his foreskin, I thought he had wounded himself from yanking on it too hard with those huge farmer hands of his. And when I saw his green eyes fall back into his head, I thought he was having some sort of a seizure like I'd seen Toto, the village idiot have out in his father's fig orchard after he fucked a chicken.

I didn't much like the sounds of romance the first time I saw jizz. I knew that Vernon was as tough as they came. Nothing frightened or threatened him. He'd cuss right in front of John Hazard, our fag Boy Scout leader as well as Miss Anderson. But when I heard him OOO and AAAh as the soap suds spit at his chest while we lay on our backs inside the pup tent, I wondered for a minute if sex wasn't actually for sissies. I tried to follow his example, but nothing would come out. With him cheering me on, saying "Harder, man. Pull on that sonofabitch. Faster, faster!" it just made matters worse. The thing went limp before the soap suds came out.

He advised me to try it more often. "Don't worry, man. It'll grow if you work on it."

When I got home the next day my mother wouldn't let me in the kitchen until I cleaned up. I was starving from being on pork and beans all weekend, so I hurried into the shower.

"Maybe if I put soap on it, just to warm up," I said to myself.

Sure enough, the bugger's big spit jumped in my eyes for the first time in my life. Every time I've heard the saying about cleanliness being next to godliness, I really get a bang.

83

Chapter Seven

The following Wednesday night I saw Vernon Knecht in the basement of the Methodist church across the street from the Del Rio Theater. Troop 42 met weekly to prepare honest young men such as myself for the fine art of tracking down Indians in the woods. I guess no one ever told my fag Boy Scout leader that we were at war with the Japs.

Vernon came up to me and said, "Hey, Jigaboo, did it grow yet?" I blushed and nodded while he rolled around on the floor laughing at me with his horse teeth stained yellow from smoking too many brown vines down by the river where he took innocent boys like me and helped them with their merit badges and physical problems.

Vernon, like all my Okie buddies, called me Jigaboo. I didn't actually look like Little Black Sambo, but like I've said, in Riverbank there were only three races of people, and the closest anyone came to being black was during the summer when brown buffalos ran practically naked in the sweltering heat of the San Joaquin Valley.

The name was not meant as an insult. It was simply a means of classification. Everyone in the Valley considers skin color to be of ultimate importance. The tone of one's pigmentation is the fastest and surest way of determining exactly who one is.

My mother, for example always referred to my father as *indio* when he'd get drunk and accuse her of being addicted to aspirin. If our neighbors got drunk at the baptismal parties and danced all night to *norteno* music, they were "acting just like Indians." Once I stuck my tongue in my sister Annie's mouth—I was practicing how to French kiss—and my ma wouldn't let me back in the house until I learned to "quit behaving like an Indian." Naturally when Bob refused to get up and salute the American flag, he was just another one of "those lazy Indians." And when my sisters began to develop their teen-age fat, as their *chi chis* expanded my mother was always after them to lay off the tortillas with hunks of colored margarine if they didn't want to end up marrying "some Indian."

In my first recorded dream I suddenly find myself crawling snake-like through the bushes toward the top of hill . . . I am on a scouting mission for the Texas Rangers. Our fort has been under seige for days. We are without food and water. All through the night we have heard their savage yells and tom-toms. Coyotes and rattlers lurk in the underbrush. I crawl carefully, my eyes in a squint just like I learned from Tom Mix. I place my ear to the ground and listen. There are at least 100 of them on horses, just due west over the ridge. I wiggle and writhe through the wild wheat. Now I'm at the crest of the small, golden hill. I ever so quietly hang my brown, narrow eyes just an inch above the grass . . . I am looking directly at the black and white eagle feathers, I cannot see the faces or the heads of the wild Indians. With grace and guts only a Boy Scout who was specially trained by Tom Mix and Vernon Knecht can muster, I gently but rapidly pluck their feathers . . . or symbols of bestiality, as Dr. Serbin said to me when I first reported the ancient dream to him.

Is it any wonder then that Vernon called me Jigaboo? Maybe if black people, righteous Negroes, had lived in Riverbank they would have been the niggers. But as things turned out, I grew up a fat, dark Mexican—a Brown Buffalo—and my enemies called me a nigger until that day I beat up Junior Ellis.

I had waited for that day for as long as I can remember. Specifically I'd been waiting ever since Halloween night of that same year—1946—when he and his brothers ambushed an entire party of Junior Perez' friends.

Perez was born on Halloween. His mother invited all the kids his age to a party that was always the social event of the fall season. I don't recall ever being invited to any other birthday party in my life. I actually went as a nigger. I rubbed my face with burnt wood. I took my mother's red rouge, painted huge lips, and borrowed my old man's white Navy gloves he kept stored with all his war equipment in case they ever called him to defend his adopted flag now that he'd become a citizen.

After we'd finished diving for apples and pinning the tail on the donkey, Perez opened his gifts. That party, like all celebrations of a particular event, was a bore. The real reason we went was for the thrill of the night march when the entire party walked the girls home. There weren't any street lights west of the Santa Fe depot. The "City of Action" could only afford street lighting and paved roads in the American sector, and they finally piped in the sewage system in the late forties only because the State threatened to cut off certain funds.

But the darkness was worth it. Mayor Hutchison will never know the experience of walking black-haired Mexican babes on Halloween night while hungry dogs howled and the village witch, La Llorona cried in search of her stolen child. I was only eleven, but I knew enough to hold on to Senaida Sanchez' warm hand while we marched in pairs through the tall weeds across the fields under a blood moon. I didn't have time to talk to Senaida, who two years later would choose me as her marching partner for the graduation exercises from grammar school. I cocked my ear towards every stray dog barking. I squinted my eyes whenever I felt a shiver up my back.

When we heard a first shriek come out of the dark we all stopped dead in our tracks. I saw several dark figures stand and shine flashlights pointed under their chins and into their eyes. Senaida grabbed my arm.

"Don't worry. It's probably Ernie," I calmed her. I figured it was some of Junior Perez' older brothers who hadn't been invited to his party.

"Are you sure?" asked the girl with the biggest breasts in Mr. White's class.

Before I could answer they were upon us. A regular ambush with whoops and shrieks and screams of blood and rape. Senaida froze. I tried to drag her along but she couldn't move until she finished pissing in her pants.

Ralph Watson, a red-faced Okie five years my senior, grabbed me by the hair and knocked me to the ground. He stood over me with his shoe on my chest. He put a flashlight to my face and screamed. "Hey, Junior, look what I got me here," he called to his partner, who had Senaida by the neck with one hand over her gorgeous cans.

The tall, skinny blond dragged her over. "What you got there, Ralph?"

Ralph kicked my balls. "Lookee here . . . I got me a fuckin nigger."

Senaida was in such shock she hadn't uttered a sound. I shouted at Junior Ellis, "You chickenshit Okie! You afraid of me?"

He pushed Senaida aside and came at me with me on my back and Ralph's foot on my crotch. Senaida still couldn't move. "Run, Sena. Run!" I screamed at her. But she wouldn't move.

"So you think I'm afraid of you, hey?" Both of them beat the shit out of me. They pulled my pants off and ripped my V-8's. I fought back, but they were too much for me. All the while they laughed and thoroughly enjoyed themselves. Ralph shined the flashlight on my crotch and said, "Whooee! Look at that. This nigger ain't even a man."

"Ain't that a fact," Junior Ellis said. "This pussy Jigaboo ain't even got hair on his prick."

With Ralph standing on each of my outstretched hands and me flat on my back, both of them spit on my hairless crotch before they ran screaming into the night with the rest of the savages. Senaida never said a word about my condition. And until this day I've not told anyone about her pissing in her pants. We nursed our wounds at her house and drank hot chocolate with *pan dulce* from Lodi's Tortilleria. When Lauren, the chief of police came to take our statements, we all said it was too dark to tell who it might have been. We hadn't lived on the West Side all our lives for nothing.

"You mean it might'a been anybody?" the tall, fat Texas Ranger said.

We all dutifully nodded our little brown heads.

"Might it of been Mesicuns?"

We shrugged and nodded without a word. That satisfied him and he left us to finish out our party. As I was leaving, Senaida accidently bumped her thirteen-year old chest into my arm. "Don't forget to wipe off your nigger-face," she said. Looking back, I might have married her if it hadn't been for Jane Addison, the pig-tailed American girl I was then hopelessly in love with.

I had been mad for Jane Addison ever since the day her father checked her into my fourth grade class at the very moment I was gazing up Miss Rollins' skirt. They were from Bend, Oregon and he'd just taken over the lumber mill two blocks from our house where my mother worked at a huge saw, cutting long pine planks into two-by-fours while my father fought the Japs.

Because of my last name, I was always given the first chair near the window in class. Everyone felt sorry for me because I couldn't sleep or sneak peeks at the comic books we smuggled in. Little did they know that from my vantage point, when we got to lay our heads on the desks while Miss Rollins read *Robinson Crusoe*, from this frontline position I could stare as long as I wanted at the long, creamy legs of the most beautiful teacher I ever had.

That day just before Jane and her father walked in she'd asked us to draw the body of a man. Unlike most brown buffalos, I couldn't draw worth a shit. The torso wasn't bad, but I just didn't know how to draw the crotch and legs. With Miss Rollins peering over my neck, I tried over and over. Finally she pulled her chair right in front of my desk and stood on it! She lifted her calf-length, purple skirt to nearly three inches above her fantastic knees.

"Now just look at my legs and try to copy them," the young woman said to me. Miss Rita Hayworth obviously didn't know that even nine-year old brown buffalos get horny when they see pure flesh. If it hadn't been for the sudden intrusion of Mr. Addison and his daughter who knows what I might have done.

Miss Rollins was cool as a cucumber. She dropped her skirt, took Jane's hand and introduced her to the class. To keep the roll in order, she made every one sitting behind me get up and move back to make room for *Addison*. Jane sat behind me for the next three years.

She was blonde, shy and had red acne all over her beautiful face. She was the smartest girl in the class and lived no more than seven blocks from me in the American sector. I never got to carry her books, but I found a new route to my house from that first day on. She didn't speak a single word to me for over a month. Then one day, during the afternoon recess she came up to me at the water fountain and said, "Do you know your mother works for my father?"

That did it. Despite her acne and the fact she got better grades than me, I knew from then on that some day we'd get married. I would work in her father's lumber mill until I proved myself. He'd make me foreman eventually and, who knows, perhaps I'd even inherit the business? The only problem would be my mother. I couldn't imagine my old ma taking orders from me.

That same night I went into the chicken coop, took my hooked knife which I used to pit peaches with, and carved her initials on the back side of my left hand . . . JA. Jane Addison. My first true love. The original *Miss It*.

I was in such a fog that I forgot to cover it with a glove or something. At supper, right in front of my mother, my brother Bob said in a loud voice, "What's that on your hand?"

I pretended not to hear. I quickly switched my fork to my right hand and put my left hand under the table.

"Hey, mom. Oscar cut himself," the bastard said.

"What?" she cried out. She couldn't stand violence unless it was part of some beating to teach me respect. "Let me see."

"It's nothing. Just a scratch," I trembled.

She grabbed at me. "Let me see, I said," she ordered.

I bent my knuckles up so the wrinkles would hide the lines of my beloved's initials. "It's just a scratch, ma."

"How'd it happen?"

"Oh, Black Panther scratched me," I heard the words come out.

The next day I asked Jane Addison if she knew my mother's name.

"Jennie, isn't it?"

"Well . . . actually, it's Juana."

She stared at me with those lovely, blue eyes. "That's a nice name."

I shuffled my feet in their black tennies and decided to seal our fate once and for all. "Did you know you have the same initials as my mother does?"

"I never thought of it . . . J-A?"

"Yep. 'Juana' is spelled with a J."

"I didn't know," the smartest girl in the class said.

I hesitated only for a moment, and then I threw it right at her. "What do you think of tatoos?"

"You mean like sailors put on their arms?"

"Yeh. Do you like them?"

"I've never seen any . . . except on Popeye," she giggled.

I thrust my left hand at her. "Ever see any like this?"

She stared hard. She nodded her head, the pigtails bobbing from side to side. "What is it? Looks like a cat scratched you."

"They're your initials, stupid!"

She squinted, gave me a queer look and just shook her head over and over as she walked away in a daze.

Even at that age, I knew that women never tell you what they really think of you. I dreamt of Jane Addison every night for two years. I'd rush through the dishes and shine my shoes before

90

my mother even finished drying them. I even quit listening to *The Shadow* on KTRB. It didn't come on until eight and by that time I was already playing basketball or riding a bike. It finally got to where I insisted on going to bed before sunset. I stopped asking for seconds at supper. My pill-head ma didn't recognize the symptoms until one night when she asked if I wanted first licks on the bowl she'd made the fudge in. I just nodded. I wasn't doing too much talking in those days. When I told her I was going to bed, she said, "Aren't you going to wait for the fudge to bake?"

"Na . . . I'm too sleepy."

"Okay, *m'hijo*. I'll bring it to you as soon as it's done."

"I don't want any," I said.

Later on I heard her tell Bob that she was worried about me. She blamed it on the war. Bob told her not to worry, that I looked better without my huge stomach. The following week she gave me five bucks to buy a violin from a friend of Bob's who had joined the marching band at Riverbank Grammar School and played the trumpet along with my brother. I kept it for a week and told her I'd rather be Benny Goodman. So she bought me a clarinet at Montgomery Ward's for thirty dollars. To the best of my knowledge, it was the first time in her life that she ever purchased something on credit.

But not even the clarinet helped. Ever since I'd shown my bleeding arms to my sweetheart we hadn't spoken a word. I'd simply decided to wait until she told me she appreciated carved tatoos. But she never did. She just ignored my obvious suffering. The pain in my gut, the secret gnawing at my belly didn't concern her one damn bit. Things got so bad for me I finally took to smoking like all my buddies were already doing. I rolled up whole pages of old funny books and smoked the shit until my lungs ached. I'd cut vines from the ivy that crawled up the sides of the chicken coop and puff on my homemade cigars until my head buzzed. On the way home from school, I'd go two blocks out of my way to pass by Lopez' Pool Hall to look for cigarette butts that the *veteranos* had flicked to the sidewalk. They had G.I. hair cuts, their old, spit-shined paratrooper boots and the same khaki uniforms they wore to fight the Japs. I'd pretend not to notice them leaning against the building. With my head down, I'd walk along the gutter and just casually push the longer butts with my toe as if I were kicking a can or a rock . . . just a barefoot boy with cheek humhumming along the road on a hot summer day in his Huckleberry Finn strides, oh yes!

Did these brave men know what I was up to? I sometimes

suspected they did. Why else would they ask me if my father had come home yet? Surely they knew the war was still on. Clearly my old man wasn't about to be released from his captivity until Tojo surrendered. FDR had finally gotten what was coming to him the year before but still they refused to set my dad free. I'm pretty sure these men understood my predicament. Why else would they throw away full inch-long Luckies and Wings? I'd kick the butt, without missing a step or crushing it, all the way to the corner, turn to see if they were looking in my direction, then pick it up and run to the little park behind the Santa Fe Depot where I kept my penny box of matches hidden in an old squirrel's nest. Then I'd light her up and suck up the hot, delicious smoke that made one a man and life barely tolerable.

Even after my old man returned from the wars with all his ribbons and a thousand stories I still struggled for survival without my love. He was so busy rigging up the house to look like a ship, printing the rules of command on little notes which he pinned to the wall above the sink, Attention: Do not waste water . . . Do not throw garbage in here; in the outhouse and in the washroom, Attention: Toilet paper rules . . . Use only four sections per use . . . Do not throw funny paper in commode. I doubt if he noticed my dying condition. When my mother threatened to divorce him if he didn't get the fuck out of the kitchen, he moved a canvas cot onto the porch and continued to instruct us there in the homilies gleaned from the *Seabee's Manual*.

One night, during a lecture from the chapter on Judo and the art of self-defense, I finally got the message. The man of wisdom was supposed to endure the agonies of waiting, maintain his balance and at the opportune moment . . . chop his enemy's fucking head off!

For two months I'd endured the humiliation of Junior Ellis' Halloween attack. Everyone in the whole school now knew that I didn't have any pubic hair. Old Watson and Junior's older brothers had even told my uncle Hector about it. He asked me if I wanted him to take care of them. Hector had lightning-fast hands. He was super cool. The best pool player in the neighborhood and the only guy I ever knew who had never lost a single game of flinch.

But I didn't want Hector's help. The day after the captain lectured us on Judo, I got my revenge on Junior Ellis on my own. It was a December morning. The last day before we went on vacation. I wouldn't see Jane until the following year. The fog had lifted and we were playing keep-away in the empty lot behind the school. As usual, the Mexicans against the Okies. And Jane

Addison sat with her best girlfriend, June Hunt, watching me rip the ball away from my enemies. Keep-away is a game without rules. There is no score. No touchdowns or home-runs. The only object is to keep the ball *away* from the other guy. Only you know if you won or if you lost.

Junior Ellis gets a pass from his younger brother, Wayne. He stands straight. No one moves toward him. He looks right at me and says, "Hey, Jigaboo. Think you're big enough to get it?"

All the others laugh. Even my buddies from the West Side understand the challenge. Everyone's eyes are upon me. I turn and see my honey looking right at me. She is wearing my favorite red skirt and white blouse. I draw in my stomach and tighten my chest. A circle begins to form. They all crowd in, leaving just enough room for us to have it out. I still haven't said a word. I walk toward him.

"What did you say?" I ask him calmly, my heart throbbing.

"I said you was a fucking, pussy-ass nigger. . . . Why?"

I keep inching up to the tall dude who's at least three years older. So long as he asks questions, I know he won't strike first. And I have learned enough from my old man to know that I mustn't swing the first blow. "I didn't hear you. Why don't you take the shit out of your mouth?"

The crowd gets a bang out of that one. Even his brother laughs at him. I can see Jane and June from the corner of my eye.

"Why, you think you can take it from me?"

"Just from you? Or from all your gang?"

The crowd roars with delight. They know exactly what I mean.

"What? You calling me yellow?" His eyes harden.

"Well, what would you call a guy who picks on girls in the dark?"

"You saying I'm chicken?" he screams at me.

I am taut. Ready for the first blow. "Yeh . . . so what of it?"

He has no choice now. I've thrown the glove down. There is no reply to the so-what-of-it? thrust. Either you strike out, then and there, or forever hold your peace.

Okies were just as tough as the Mexicans. They were as mean in street-fighting as any greaser in our turf. And so we went to it. "Why, you fucking black nigger!" he shouted as he tore into me. A push, a shove and an uppercut right to the button. You go right for the face. Tear into his eyes. Rip his nose off. Kick him in the shins, in the groin, wherever you can land. On the ground you scratch his face, rub dirt in his eyes, anything. People yell, scream and cheer you on. You don't think of your clothes or the soreness you know you'll feel for the next couple of days. It doesn't matter that you bleed over yourself, that you actually get closer to a man than at any other time in your life. The adrenalin does most of the work for you. You are in such a state of insanity that only death, a knock-out or his surrender will stop you . . .

I whipped Junior Ellis good on that last day before we went on our Christmas vacation. And no Okie sonofabitch ever called me a nigger to my face ever again. Only Vernon Knecht and some other friends called me Jigaboo as a nickname to remind me of my victory. The fight won, I walked right past Jane Addison without so much as looking in her direction.

After the recess Miss Anderson read adventure stories to us. She had short hair and tits the size of pillows. Ever since she had come to my defense in the first grade, I looked upon her as one of the few Americans I could trust. She told the others that even President Roosevelt's children wore short pants. "It's part of the war effort, children. Our men need the material to bandage the wounded." Naturally the following week some of the pussy-faced, apple-polishers came to school in their own patriotic short pants.

When we returned to class on that day I was covered with bumps on my head, bruises on my arms, sweat just poured and mixed with the dirt. My heart still pounded madly as Miss Anderson began to read Perry Mason. "If you boys want, you can take off your shirts. It's just too hot today."

I peel off my torn shirt. I lay my aching head in my bloody arms. Like all good street fighters, I carefully reconstruct the entire fight to see if I made any mistakes. Every word, every gesture leading up to the first blow goes through my throbbing head.

Suddenly I feel a foot touch the heel of my tennies. What is this? Who else but *Miss It*? Can it really be true? Has she finally come around? Two years, and now at last she answers the throb of my tatoo . . . or was it an accident?

And again. A little tap. Close to a kick. Miss Anderson's voice goes on and on about that famous criminal lawyer who always gets his man. Is it really happening to me? I lightly kick back to let her know I got her message.

"Yes, Jane. What is it?" I hear my teacher say.

Silence . . . my heart flutters butterflies. My God!

"Will you please ask Oscar to put on his shirt? . . . He stinks."

The room is filled with laughter. My ears pound red. I am done for. My heart sags from the overpowering weight of the fatness of my belly. I *am* the nigger, after all. My mother was right. I am nothing but an Indian with sweating body and faltering tits

94

that sag at the sight of a young girl's blue eyes. I shall never be able to undress in front of a woman's stare. I shall refuse to play basketball for fear that some day I might have my jersey ripped from me in front of those thousands of pigtailed, blue-eyed girls from America.

I keep my eyes closed tightly so that no one will see my tears. I put on my torn, bloody shirt. Even as Miss Anderson continues the story of Perry Mason I leave my dead head in my arms and cast myself into the iron jaws of her father's saw . . . dressed up in fine linen, my hands folded over my chest, a rosary in the delicate fingers, I await my maker in a golden, finely carved casket which shall be my resting place throughout eternity. There they sit, all of them: my folks, her folks, Bob, Hector, all my cousins, my grandmother, Vernon, the Perez', Miss Anderson and, of course *Miss It* . . . suddenly she gives a tremendous shriek. She jumps up, runs to the front of the church, takes the rosary from my carved-up, bleeding hands and bends to kiss the little holes in my hands. Even in death I can feel the warmth of her lovely tears.

"Look, Mrs. Acosta! Look at his hands. See? These are *my* initials . . . J-A. Joan Anderson. That's me. He truly loved me!"

. . . "You never mentioned that to me," my Jewish shrink says, jumping into the front seat of the fleeting green Plymouth at ninety miles an hour. How dare the pig interrupt my fond memories just when I was getting to the good part.

"Bullshit! I told you about her." I am pissed. My eyes are on the road. Here I am far north into, what'd the last sign say? Idaho?

"Hey, lighten up," I hear what sounds like the voice of Ted Casey. But I can't get a good look, the beer and the bennies in my head get in the way.

"What the fuck are you doing in here?"

"No, Mr. Acosta, I meant you never said anything about that fantasy about your death," Serbin says.

"What fantasy? What the fuck are you talking about?"

The Owl pours it on. "That ain't no fantasy, you dumb kike. You ought to get to know your patients a little better."

Because Dr. Serbin is a professional, he does not answer.

Chapter Eight

I see her sitting on her pack, her legs slightly ajar, next to an open field on the outskirts of Ajax, northern Nevada. I shift her down and slow to a stop. I look through the open window and wait for the young chick to move. Levis and long blonde hair, she gazes past my window. It is the dawn of a new day at three in the afternoon. Twenty years of driving and I have never been so lucky. I casually light up a Camel.

"Want a ride?" Steve McQueen calls to the broad.

Without so much as a trace of fear of the brown beast, she says, "How far you going?"

"I'm just driving."

She stands and I swallow. Long legs, a perfect ass and a smile to melt your heart out. She casts the scout pack into the rear with the elan of a rich, hippie chick without a trace of a smudge. Before she can change her mind I get her up to ninety.

"Do you have anymore of that?" She points to my beer.

"Doesn't everybody?" My heart pounds madly.

I turn the radio up full blast and Jesus Christ, motherfucker, sonofabitch, chickenshit, cocksucker, dirty toad, there it is again! The bastard has me by the neck. My ears pour out buckets of adrenalin and I am hooked to those "cartwheels on the floor . . ."

By the time we reached Sun Valley, Karin Wilmington knew my life story. I am not a man to hide things. My deepest secrets, my unkindest thoughts I reveal immediately to strangers. I've-got-a-story-and-I've-got-a-song-and-if-you-want-to-ride-along-with-me, well, you've-just-got-to-go-along, my amphetamine-ridden brain rails on and on. I believe I even told her about Jane Addison and my old man's motorcycle hangup. I must have told her about Russel Tansey's iguana, because when I got to the part about Trader JJ's she began to ask questions.

"And this guy who rode the motorcycle through the bar had a cast on his *left* leg? A full, up-to-the-hip cast?"

"Yeh, he's a poet of sorts," I pouted, not appreciating the interruption.

"Could his name be Turk?" the rich blonde asked with her blue eyes aflame.

"Nah, his name's John." Shit, here it comes, I thought. And just as we were getting warm. But what the hell, fate can't drag up the world that tight. "He's from Chicago . . ."

"Right! John Tibeau!" the girl squealed in delight. "We call him Turk."

" 'We?' Who's that?"

"His wife, his friends, all of us call him Turk. Didn't you know he used to live in Sun Valley?"

As things turned out, she was a friend of his wife, another rich girl from Idaho. It seems that John insisted they ride his motorcycle to their wedding. After the ceremony he got on his bike and rode the blasted machine around the dance floor until his new father-in-law told the bride he'd expected more than a Hell's Angel to inherit his millions. The best man was a writer who'd just published a book on the motorcycle outlaws after riding with them for a year. Together they rode bareback into the table of gifts, then they drove up the mountain outside Ketchum where they crashed into Hemingway's grave.

"That sounds like one of John's stories," I said as we approached a little town at the foot of some pine-coned mountains. It was barely dawn.

"I know. But I got it from Michael. He tends bar right down that street," she said pointing. "In fact . . . look, can you stop for a moment?"

This is it, I thought. I knew that God damned Tibeau would interfere even up here. I just wanted to drop her and be on my way.

"You've got no place to stay, right?"

"I'm not planning to *stay* anywhere."

"But, dear you've been on the road for, what did you say, two days?"

"Yeh . . . two or three. I really can't tell."

"And I'll bet you haven't eaten."

"Well, there's lots of food in this Bud."

She smiled at that old alcoholics' excuse. "I just don't know about you, dear . . . no plans, no food, no sleep. What are you *doing* to yourself? Are you becoming a hippie?"

"A hippie?" I shouted. "Hey, I told you I was a lawyer, for Christ sake."

"Yes, I know, dear. But wouldn't you say you were, how do they say, 'Dropping Out'?"

She had told me her father owned a million acres of Idaho potatoes. When I told her my family used to be into corn and onions, she decided we had something more than John Tibeau in common. She really wasn't the hippie chick I'd picked up twelve hours ago. She was merely a rich, beautiful broad with more class than I could muster on July the fourth, 1967. How in the fuck would a brown buffalo stick a dirty dick into a classy broad that called him dear? What was I to do with a potato farmer's daughter who'd just hitchhiked from Ketchum to Frisco to Mexico City to Acapulco and back? And with something like a million bucks in her sheepskin jacket.

Of course she was right. The rich and the beautiful are always right. They can see it without the dust you find in a brown buffalo's eyes. I've yet to know a winner lose. Isn't that why I went to law school in the first place? And now, here I am, just a fucking buffalo on the lam. *Dropping out with Timothy Leary.*

What a fucking joke . . . I used to know the old fag when I studied General Semantics with Dick Dettering at S.F. State in the late fifties. Dick was a friend of Betty's before I ran into her at Modesto State Hospital where I worked as a recreational therapist assistant for the insane. The broad was from St. Louis. She taught mental patients how to make leather goods so they wouldn't spend all their time jacking off. She actually had a degree in the fine art of occupational therapy.

Anyway, Betty took me by the hand and drove me to Frisco to teach me culture and the finer things in life. We ended up

99

at Dicko's pad in Twin Peaks and got drunk on Red Mountain. He was the co-editor with S.I. Hayakawa of *ETC.*, the magazine put out by those word freaks. He had it all over that short, stubby gruff who got all the glory. Yes, I'm one of the few people in the world who actually knows that Don Hayakawa got a lot of his ideas from Dicko. This, of course was years before he became a friend of Ronald Reagan, the movie star.

The first time I met Hayakawa I told him that my father had been a crew member of the *Enola Gay.* He turned his back to me, went to the piano and played "Tea For Two."

When Dicko discovered I shared his feelings about the short Jap, we became the best of friends. He introduced me to all the intellectuals at S.F. State and convinced me I should be a writer since I had so many fucking stories to tell. Little did he know I was scared shitless of all those guys with the tweed coats and fancy pipes. He'd invite Van Tilburg Clark, Mark Harris, Herb Gold and other twirps to his pad and get them all drunk on good old Red Mountain.

These guys weren't the world famous fags they are today. In fact, most of them were alive then. Even Tim Leary was still on this earth. He hadn't learned to walk on water at the time. He was into rats and monkeys. He tried his best to explain to me the importance of sticking little electrical jabs in their brains to find out what was in the human head.

Since I was about ten years younger than this crew of alcoholics, I just listened and filled their cups with cheap wine. After they'd had enough, I'd tell them of my escapades in Riverbank and in Panama where I'd worked with the Southern Baptist Convention and Jesus Christ to save the black souls of niggers, spics and Indians. I used to keep my eye on Harris when I told my stories. He had this nasty habit of pulling out a little notebook in the middle of a conversation and jotting down, as he said, "story ideas."

Later on, after I'd transferred to S.F. State and taken his writing course, he asked me if I wanted to read his first draft of *Wake Up, Stupid!* I kept it for a week and returned it to him at the next short story seminar. I only read the first paragraph. After that, I was no longer afraid of the intellectuals. I knew I could tell a better story. All I said was "It's pretty good, man." He quit coming over to Dick's after that.

Seven years later, in the spring of '67, I ran into Tim Leary at Golden Gate Park. Charlie Fisher had an old Fagel Bus. We drove it to the panhandle to listen to Jerry Garcia and The Grateful Dead in the first round of those Love-Ins the hippies had in the late 60's. The Fagel was an ancient house-bus, with hardwood sides and an inside toilet. Every manner of freak stood or sat on top of the brown bus while Country Joe whomped on "The Masked Marauder." From out of nowhere, old Tim floated down to us through the eucalyptus wearing a white gown. He was all teeth by then. The crowd forgot about The Fish and immediately ganged up around the bus. Their savior was inspecting the beast. Charlie Fisher is not impressed with famous people. He has tons of bread stored in the Republican bank of Devil's Lake, North Dakota, so he didn't need anything Timothy had to offer. He showed him around and said, "Listen, if you haven't a place to stay, you're welcome to crash in here. I'm gonna leave it parked right here in case anyone needs a place to rest."

Tim didn't say a word. He was so fucked up I doubt he knew of his own existence. I walked up to him and said, "Hey, Tim! You old bastard, how you doing?"

He stared right past and showed me a mouthful of white teeth. I knew right then and there that religion and hard drugs just don't mix. So I couldn't take his message to heart. I just went back to my blue television and freaked out on Procol Harum three months later . . .

I open my eyes when I hear a horse snorttle. I'm leaning against the window. A cowboy in leather and brass is riding by. I am alone. Karin has left me without a word in the middle of the little tourist village where Ernest Hemingway is buried. There are cowboys, young girls in short pants and Tony Lama boots. Everything is yellow and green. I had expected to see millions of potatoes. When we'd pulled into Ketchum it was barely dawn. Now it is mid-day. And she is gone. But what's this? A little note stuck between the fingers of a bobby-pin on the sun visor.

> Dear Mr. Hawk . . . You fell asleep. When you rest up, come to visit us. We have some wonderful potato juice. Call me at Carl Wilmington's . . . Peace & Love.
>
> Karin

Who in the hell is Hawk? . . . Ah, yes. I'd told her my name was Henry Hawk after she told me she knew Tibeau. No sense in taking any chances. And when she started telling me about her trip to Mexico City . . . I hate for people to assume I'm an authority on Mexicans. Just because I'm a brown buffalo doesn't mean I'm the son of Moctezuma, does it? Anyway, I told her I was a Samoan by the name of Henry Hawk. That made it much easier for her to tell me what she really thought of Mexico. Something about beach boys down in Acapulco and their wonderful tobacco . . . I revved up the green Plymouth and went to look for a bar. I was dirty and my Budweiser was gone.

"You from around these parts?" the fat, pimple-faced cowboy asked when he brought me a beer.

"Nah, I'm from Oklahoma," I said with my best Lee Marvin accent. Fortunately I had changed into my Levis and construction boots back in Elko, Nevada. The best I could do was cut the sleeves of my $7.95 Arrow shirt with my pocket knife. As a lawyer, I didn't have too many cowboy outfits. But the bennies and the booze had given me a raw look. Three days without food had melted some of the fat away.

The cowboy nodded. "Cherokee?"

"Nah, Blackfoot," Lee Marvin replied.

"That's what I figured. Get lots of them up around these parts."

"You got yourself a nice little town here," I said.

"It's pretty good. The tourists won't be here for a while yet."

"Yeh, I hear you got some good hunting up around these parts."

"You a hunter?" he asked.

"Not this trip."

"Looking for work, are you?" the cowboy said.

"Nope. I'm on business."

"Monkey business," he forced a laugh.

"Nah, buffalos," I threw back at him and sipped on my thirty-third beer.

He stepped back lightly. Narrowing his eyes, he said, "Buffalos?"

"Yeh. We raise buffalos. On my way to Wyoming to pick up a few bulls."

"Oh, I see," he said relieved. "What, you the foreman?"

"Chief . . . my tribe holds the deed. But I guess the Bureau owns it all."

"Yeh, shit. Same as my bar here . . . the bank owns it all."

He walked away to serve another customer. An old whiskey-faced woman in Levis and cowboy boots said to him, "Gimme another snort, Harry." Soon he was back for more.

"So you're a chief? I mean, a *real chief.*"

"Well, I ain't got no feathers. But I'm the head man, yeh."

He belched a good, hard laugh, slapping the bar with a wet towel. He said to the woman, "Did you hear that one, Hazel? Feller here says he's a chief . . . but he ain't got no feathers." He shook his head and blurted some whooeeys and God damns under his boisterous laugh. The woman waited a second, looked at me, and then smiled. The cowboy stepped toward her and said, "Says he's looking for buffalos."

"Buffalos?"

'Yeh, he's a chief of some . . . Blackfoot was it?"

I nodded to both of them and gave them my best oh-shucks smile.

"And he's going to Wyoming to look for some buffalo. . . . Can you beat that?"

The old woman leaned toward me. "Kind of off the road for Wyoming, aren't you?"

I figured I'd misjudged her. I can usually tell a cowboy or an Okie the minute he opens his mouth. But she had fooled me by the way she ordered her shot of whiskey. I had absolutely no idea where Wyoming or Oklahoma was in relation to wherever we were. When I'd left Frisco, I decided on one simple guide: no maps. No plans of any kind whatsoever. Just head the car away from the TRO's and Dr. Serbin. But I can think in a pinch. My horsetrader father had taught me well.

"I'm just stopping to visit some friends."

"You got friends here in Ketchum?" The old bitch continued. I knew then for sure I hadn't fooled her with my Indian joke.

"Well, sort of. I met them in Cuba some time ago. . . . You ever heard of Hemingway? The writer?"

The cowboy suddenly stopped wiping the glass. He gave the woman a close-in look. "You're a friend of Mary's?"

"Not exactly. I used to work for *Mr.* Hemingway. I doubt she'd remember me. I used to drive him around Havana when he was down there. . . . It's been a long time."

The cowboy said, "I guess you know he had an accident a couple of years back."

"Oh, sure. I read about it. . . . To tell you the truth, he treated me real well; and I just wanted to stop by and pay my respects . . . you know, visit the grave and leave some flowers." We were silent for a minute. I was pretty sure I had the cowboy, but the woman wasn't convinced. I lowered my voice, squinted my eyes and puckered my lips for the right effect. "It's kind'a personal . . . I was in the Air Force, stationed at Guantanamo. I was moonlighting, driving tourists around. I speak Spanish . . . anyway, my wife got sick and he lent me the money to fly back to the States. I can't say I really *knew* him, but he was damned nice to me when I had some real troubles . . . a man doesn't forget a thing like that."

It worked. I thought I spotted a tear on the old boozer's wrinkled cheek.

"Well, listen, son. Mary comes in here pretty regular. But she isn't feeling too well just right now."

"Mrs. Hemingway, you mean?" I threw in for good measure.

"Yeh, she's got a touch of the flu or something," she said.

The cowboy was completely sucked in. "You can visit the old man's grave. It's just down this road, north about, oh, a mile or so."

"And there's a monument down by the river," the old woman said. "Go straight out east past the ski lifts. Lots of tourists like to visit."

I stood up, and decided to make my getaway before I fucked up. I knew the beer was getting to me. It was time for another handful of bennies. "Well, my God, I'm in luck. I thought I'd have a hell of a time finding anything. All's he ever told me was the name of the town. And I read he'd been buried right around here."

"We wouldn't have it no other way," the cowboy said. I reached over to shake his hand. "Thanks a lot, mister. I appreciate it."

"No trouble at all, Chief. My pleasure."

I nodded to the woman and started to walk out. She said, "Say, young man, what's your name? I'll tell Mary you stopped by."

I was right at the door and I knew I could make it, so I said, "She wouldn't know it . . . but Mr. Hemingway used to call me Brown Buffalo. Just tell her the Brown Buffalo stopped to pay his respects."

I drove north toward the cemetery past the little ranches with shingled roofs. It was a simple, flat burial ground for the local citizens of Ketchum. A lazy gardener with his eye on the upkeep had designed a large lawn without flowers or trees as the old man's resting place. A simple slab of stone with his name chiseled into the rock is all that holds Papa down under. I took a bunch of yellow chrysanthemums from a neighboring grave and placed them over his head. Careful not to step on him, I sat beside his bed and waited for his message on this sunny, warm afternoon . . .

Chapter Nine

All through grammar school my old man had said to me, "You do what I say until you're fourteen. That's when I left home and started taking care of myself. You obey me until then and then you'll be on your own." So on my fourteenth birthday I walked into the house smoking a pipe and my mother slapped me smack in the face, knocking the pipe to the floor. I picked it up and stuck it back in my mouth. "I'm fourteen today, mom. Today's my birthday."

She slapped me again and said, "I don't care if you're forty! You're not going to smoke in front of me!"

"But I had a deal with my dad. He said I could do what I wanted. He's always told me that."

"Then go smoke in front of him, *malcriado*! You're going to respect me or I'll slap you till it hurts."

I picked up the pipe and held it in my hand. "But, mom. It doesn't hurt anymore."

She slapped me again and I simply smiled at her. Tears swelled in her eyes and the romance was over. She ran into her bedroom and cried until my father came home. It was April the eighth, 1949 and I was about to complete my first year of high school. (I had been enrolled in the first grade a year early, my mother had lied to the teacher because she couldn't afford a babysitter and had to work in the fields with my father. Because of my size no one had questioned my age. The following year, on April the eighth, 1942, Miss Anderson announced to the class that it was my birthday, and that I was now seven years old. I corrected her and insisted I was only six. It was the only time I argued with Miss Anderson. She took me to the principal and they finally called in my mother who admitted to them that she had lied. So I was always the youngest one in my class all through school. I was also the biggest.)

My father held true to his promise. After my fourteenth birthday I was allowed to be on my own. But I had the good sense not to push it. Besides, what would a woman know of such things as smoking and drinking and carousing around. But I could stay out and go where I wanted as long as I didn't throw it in her face and maintained the proper respect. Since most freshmen at Oakdale Joint Union High School did not have similar bargains with their fathers, I started to hang around with the older guys I knew on the football team and the band, my two principal occupations during high school when I wasn't working at the Pink Elephant, the beer bar my father and uncle owned my last three years of school.

For six months my father and his brother Tony had argued nightly about what kind of business they would purchase with their G.I. loans. For two months they went over plans for a grocery store, which they finally decided would make no money because the Spaniard, Bordona had all the barrio trade sewed up with his West Side Grocery right across the street from the house we had moved into. Then they talked night after night about a pool hall, before deciding that Lopez' Pool had the corner on that trade. Finally they heard that the Army was selling all the barracks at Camp Beal in Marysville, so for nine months we spent our weekends going to that small town in northern California to tear out equipment and lumber from what used to be an officer's mess hall during the Second World War and building the Pink Elephant, which went into bankruptcy four years later because my father was an Indian from the mountains of Durango and could not hold his booze.

He'd open around noon and by the time I'd come in from school to take over, he'd be exchanging tall stories with Chihuahau

106

or some other friend from Durango and putting it all on the tab which never quite managed to get paid. I took my pay out in trade. After my fourteenth birthday I had access to all the beer, corn chips, Polish sausages and pigs' feet me and my buddies could consume. We'd simply back the car into the storage room and load her up for the evening's action.

The Fearless Four, as we called ourselves, went cruising Tenth Street in Modesto, circling Burgi's Drive Inn or dragging the Okies along the canal banks with the trunk loaded with Goebel beer every night for three years. We searched for snatch in the highlands and the low. We whistled, honked, flirted and smart-talked every cunt we found on the streets. But I must confess that in three years of pussy-chasing the Fearless Four never made a single score. Instead we became alcoholics before I graduated from Oakdale Joint. During those years, between 1948 and June of 1952, I didn't know or even hear of one single dope user. The only action on the street was booze and hot cunt. And although I was first string on the football team, first soloist in the reed section of the concert and dance bands and president of my class, I never had a girl friend and I never scored any chick in school or on the streets.

We called Tim Watkins "Dragalong," because he broke his leg against the Manteca Bulldogs when he tried an illegal "kidney-block" and missed. That same game I had been kicked out because they caught me rubbing dirt in the quarterback's eyes during a pile up. Bob Whitt and I would exchange. First I'd pull some dirty stunt like accidentally stepping on their balls as I got up from a tackle. After being warned by the officials I'd cool it while Whitt would stick his fingers up someone's nose knowing the referee would have his eyes on me. All three of us got booted that game, the championship for the Valley Oak League . . . it ended up a three-way tie for first along with Ceres because they called back our touchdown when they caught Dragalong flying through the air with his knee aimed right at the fullback's kidney.

In the locker room after the game we salted our wounds and let the tears flow freely to show our commitment. Joe Sigfried, our coach who once played with the Chicago Bears asked quietly, "What's this I hear that you guys have been playing dirty?" He looked straight at the three of us. "I've tried to teach you bastards good sportsmanship and now I'm under fire because they've got movies of you three doing some chickenshit thing or another!" He gave us the meanest look a coach can give his boy. And then he whispered, "Next time, you idiots, hit 'em harder but don't get caught."

107

That night we drank cases of beer and a bottle of gin during the dance in the gym which honored the heroes. But, then, as every other night, none of us could pick up a broad. Perhaps it was our reputation for being the biggest drunks in school. Or the fact that everyone knew that the real reason we called Tim Watkins Dragalong was not because of his cast, but because he had a ten inch cock, when soft. In any event, Ben Hill was on leave from the Navy that weekend so we split the dance early and drove up the hills to Jamestown, an old mining town with five whorehouses we visited monthly. Our favorite was Ruby's Banana Ranch.

I was a junior, fifteen years old and except for a minor skirmish with a cousin at the age of twelve, I had never been fucked. I had always gone along with the other three, but I had held fast. The broads were fantastic and they all tried desperately to get me into bed so they could claim a cherry, but I was waiting for my beloved and it sure as hell wasn't going to be some old whore, no matter how much I ached, itched and splattered the stuff in the shower.

The summer of my twelfth year I had made a promise to God that if my cousin didn't spill the beans on me, I'd keep that nasty thing in my pants until I married. She was a bit younger, but had already learned the ropes when she asked me if I wanted to learn the tricks of the trade. Everything was going well until we heard a knock on the door. My brother Bob hollered for us to open. We maintained and he shouted, "I know what you guys are doing. Open up!" After he left, she got right back to it. But it wouldn't expand. It wouldn't budge an inch no matter how hard we tried. She blamed it on me, naturally, and said, "You must never leave a girl with a tickle like I've got . . . now do it or I'll tell my dad."

So for six months I refused to visit any relative, and for six months I suffered, suffocated, choked and sweated every hour of the day. I turned to God and prayed hourly. In bed, in the shower, at school, at the Boy Scout meetings, out in the orchards and in my tree house where I still maintained vigil in case the enemy broke the treaty. Everywhere and at all times I promised Him for six months that no matter what happened, if He would keep her mouth shut, I'd save my cherry for my bride.

Who knows how long I would have stayed a virgin had it not been for my brother's confession? Some six months after my first aborted lay, he told me that after I had left my cousin's house that night, he had returned to find her still under the covers with this great itch—which he satisfied by doing the dirty deed. But

I was the captain's son! A deal is a deal, no matter what, and I had sworn to remain a virgin. Had it not been for Ruby, who knows what would have become of me.

Ruby was the madam of the Banana Ranch. She was a knockout. None of us had ever seen her go into a room. She greeted you, took you into the red-velveted parlor and poured whatever you wanted. One's age played no role in this liberal cathouse. "If they can pay, they can play," she was fond of telling all the high school kids we brought around. She wore regular street clothes and colored stockings. For some reason, this made her more desirable than the broads whom she paraded in, two at a time per customer, who wore various costumes or none at all. We'd dance and drink and try desperately to hold back until Ruby's girls threatened to leave for the men in the other rooms.

Try as they might, I had kept myself out of those private rooms for a year and a half. Ruby would protect me. When she saw the girls were getting to me pulling at my pants, sticking their tongues up my ears and goosing me in the ass until my eyes were flooded, she'd send them out. She'd pour me a free drink and tell me, "I don't blame you, Oscar. I wouldn't want my son to give his cherry to some tramp either."

But, God how I itched. No one will ever know my absolute aching for just a crack at one of those hussies. Ruby was so fantastic I wouldn't dare to dream of her. But when she'd sit next to me, her dress up to her knees and her Portuguese tits hanging in front of me . . . Christ! When the record played Johnny Ray, "If Your Sweetheart Sends A Letter Of Goodbye," Ruby would toast a drink, lifting her glass to my face . . . shit! When the record stopped, it was quiet. I could hear the thump-thump-thump in the next room where Dragalong had entered with the Italian broad that tried to pick on me first . . . at times I almost had to forceably restrain myself from crashing into that room and ripping her apart with my bare hands.

After the dance in the gym, that Friday night we tied Manteca, as we raced towards the Banana Ranch, Ben the sailor with the big head beamed at us and said, "Treat's on me."

"It's about time you broke your cherry," the Okie with the penguin's nose said to me. Bob Whitt looked like a young Jimmy Stewart and acted like my father all those years we ran around looking for snatch.

"Yeh, Jigaboo, it's time. The guys on the team are beginning to wonder about it," Dragalong said.

"I haven't said no," I said.

"And you haven't said yes," Ben Hill said.

"Now, Oscar," Whitt began to unwind as he opened another Goebel. "You know you got to have a go at it sometime. Why not tonight? We're beginning to catch hell from that pimp that runs Ruby's joint."

"Yeh, we can't just let you go in and get a look forever," Ben said.

They railed hard on me all the way to Jamestown. By the time we got up there I was loaded to the gills. We could drink more beer than any team of four I'd known in my life. Two cases a night was nothing.

We entered and immediately Dragalong went into the rear with Ruby. When they returned, Ruby was in a red negligee. Just red lips, red cheeks and yellow perfume over her olive complexion. She was Portuguese and had the finest knockers of the bunch. I was astounded. I've never seen her in a costume. All three of my friends went into other rooms within a few minutes. I was in a sweat. "The Wheel Of Fortune" was spinning by when she sat next to me on the couch and told me with heavy tears that her son had just been drafted.

"I'm so lonely, so sad, you just can't imagine," she blubbered as she leaned into me with those choice, delectable, sumptuous breasts. I wiggled as she casually ran her red fingernails up and down my back while she told me another sad story of how her boss had told her she'd have to start hustling again because she had allowed too many high school kids to sit and drink free booze while they pretended to be making up their minds about which whore to take to the rooms. "I just don't know what to do, my friend."

"Did he mention *me*?" I asked.

"It doesn't matter, Oscar. I told him you were my favorite customer. I said, 'He's my friend. He's not just a customer. And besides, he brings in trade even if he does have . . .' uh, well, you know . . . I told him you were studying for the priesthood."

"I'm not going to be a God damn priest, Ruby! What'd you say that for?"

"Well, I'm sorry, dear . . . but he accused you of . . . you know, he said you were . . . sissy. The bastard actually tried to tell me you were a homosexual. Can you beat that?"

She leaned into my ear and gave me a soft, gingery kiss. I couldn't take it any more. Her Jergen's lotion was just more than I could handle! I grabbed her breast and plunged full blast into her mouth. "That motherfucker thinks I'm a punk? He said that?"

110

"Oh, don't pay any attention to him. I understand, honey."

I got up and pulled her right up. Those Portuguese, long-lashed eyes had troubled me long enough. "Fuck God and fuck the Pope," I commanded as I led her into her own private bedroom.

There she taught me all there is to know about Around the World. I had already finished twice when I heard a giggle. I looked between my legs as I lay on my back, with Ruby on her knees above me, and I saw Dragalong peering through a curtain of colored beads which led into the kitchen. "Go to it, Oscar! Give it to her again!"

On our way back to the Valley, they told me it had all been a setup. I didn't mind, for I had at last gotten God off my back after suffering for two years with the itch. I kept going back for more business every month for the next year until I met Alice.

The four of us were parked along the canal bank one night near Riverbank, drinking beer when Bob Whitt asked me, "You planning to go back to school in September?" It was the summer of 1951, Ben Hill was home on leave again, Dragalong had just gotten out of basic training for the weekend and Bob Whitt was by now a serious alcoholic. I had one more year to go at Oakdale Joint Union and I'd already been Class President, the top musician in the school, and first string tackle on the Varsity for two years. So the summer doldrums, a season of ennui, had already crept into our nightly drinking sessions.

"Why don't you join the Navy," Ben asked.

"You can probably get into the band, Jigaboo," Dragalong said.

"Nah, I might as well finish . . . besides, who knows, maybe this year will be different."

"Shit, there's nothing happening," Whitt, the dropout, said.

I don't know about that," Dragalong said. "My sister's starting high school this year, and, man, she's got some wild friends. I just saw them today. They went on some Girl Scout trip, and I tell you, if I was still around . . ."

And once again, for the seventeen millionth time we started going over the list of broads in the entire San Joaquin Valley. We didn't merely undress them, we measured and weighed every ounce of flesh, we picked their clothes for them, sent them to the beauty shop, brushed their teeth if we thought it necessary, combed, bathed and even manicured the girls and women of the Valley before we sent them to school, to work or to someone's bed. And always there was but one objective: to find the perfect woman. *Miss It.* To find the proper object of our affection, the dream of our collec-

111

tive design, the flower for our garden, the pin-up for our wall and the one we could all agree we would marry when the time was ripe. And on that hot, summer night after we had dipped into the canal for a quick swim while we worked on a case of Goebel's, Dragalong told us of Alice, a friend of his sister, a thirteen year-old farmer's daughter from Riverbank whom he had just met that day and who would be a freshman at Oakdale Joint that fall.

"She is the cat's meow. I'm telling you. Cans up to her chin and an ass like a brick shithouse. I've never seen a better looking snatch in my whole life."

We drove to Clause Road and waited for the sun to rise. Tim Watkins was going to prove to us that Alice was in fact our *Miss It*, the woman we had all sought for three years. While the cows trekked into the barn and the crows sought out their pickings from the freshly-cut clover, the four hoodlums sat huddled in my old, souped up black and grey '34 Ford and waited for the farmer's daughter to appear. After two hours she came out into the yard behind the house and walked with a limp into the barn. I only saw her for a moment but I knew she was the one. It was instant love after only the brief sight of a face of peach, an aura of almond blossoms and the grace of a floating dove on a summer morning of 1951. I said absolutely nothing to my friends. My ears burned when I heard them profane her lovely body, but I held it all in check. I didn't want to give them any reason to prevent me from getting to her later.

Korea caught up three of the Fearless Four and I went back to school alone, played football and clarinet and fought with my teachers. I was a senior, and at last beginning to think of something other than Goebel beer along canal banks. After I had been elected Jr. Class President, I had forgotten about being a brown buffalo. When I became the solo clarinetist and played the lead role in *Captain From Castille* I quit hanging around with Johnny and David and Ben and Alfonso, my grade-school buddies from the West Side, because they constantly talked about the gringos and the Okies and the Americans and all kinds of things that I could not accept as true since for me all was going king ass.

I never went out with the few Mexican girls in school because they always stuck to themselves and refused to participate in the various activities. Also they were square and homely. Even when my mother asked me one time why I didn't go out with Rita or Senaida, I told her that they weren't "my type," they always held back, eating their lunch under the shed for the bicycles instead of on the lawn with "the rest of the people." I made no judgments upon Mexican girls in general, for I had been raised a proud brown buffalo, but the seven Chicanas that went on to Oakdale Joint Union were, quite simply, a drag. "You'll change your mind one of these days," my mother said to me. But I didn't for twenty years. All through school, in the Air Force, in San Francisco and in Alpine, I did not know one Mexican girl that aroused the beast within me.

I started drinking more. I made no attempt to find a girlfriend. And after a time I even quit going to see Ruby.

I never studied once all through high school. I was a music major and so all I ever did was practice my clarinet. I always had some girl do my homework and write my term papers. For exams I would cheat. Either I'd steal the test beforehand, write certain facts and formulas on my arm, or simply ask Barbara or Peggy to move their arms or their heads so I could copy. One day Mrs. Russell caught me stealing glances at Barbara's exam. But that kind of cheating is the most difficult thing in the world to prove. "I was thinking," I said when she accused me. Since Barbara sat in front of me, it was perfectly natural for me to think with my eyes open staring straight ahead.

But Mrs. Russell had it in for me. I knew I'd be punished. I'd gotten away with too much in the past. Several weeks before I had found a small vial, a plastic bottle for pills when I was cleaning up the bar. I filled it with powdered chickenfeed. Going into class one morning, I dashed a few specks on Madeline Hart's Popsicle. She cried out and I told her, "Eat it. You need the stuff to make your tits grow." Because she had not yet grown and perhaps because she had a secret yearning for me, the short Dutch girl came on like a kid and told Mrs. Russell.

"What did you throw on her Popsicle?" she demanded.

"Spanish Fly," I said innocently.

"Spanish Fly? What's that?" the pregnant teacher from Waterford asked.

"We feed it to our chickens. It makes them lay more eggs."

"Chickens? Is it poisonous?"

"No, of course not. It's just mashed corn with something they get from the rooster. There's nothing wrong with it. I used to eat it all the time. Want to try it?"

She let it go at that. The next day she asked me to stay after. "I just want to tell you . . . I asked my husband about your 'chickenfeed' and . . . now I know why they say what they do about . . . filthy minded boys like you." Her blue eyes flared in disgust. She was pregnant and for a moment I worried she'd drop it if I didn't apologize.

113

She never forgot. So the day she caught me cheating she kicked me out of class and sent me to study hall. When I walked into the large room with a hundred students hard at work, I was relieved. The overseer was Mayer Corrigan, a short, fat music teacher who had taught me all I knew. He was way up front for my favorite teacher role. He was a terrific trumpet player, even though his lip was partially paralyzed by a Jap bullet during World War II. He could write the music out that he heard on a phonograph without having to repeat it. I played in the high school dance band, a jazz band when people still thought that Stan Kenton was a communist and that anyone who liked progressive music, who actually listened to Gerry Mulligan or Chet Baker, must be some sort of dope addict. Whenever the band went on the road, he'd let us smoke in the bus and tell us, "Just don't get drunk before we begin."

Mayer just laughed when I told him the story about the Spanish Fly. He told me to either take a seat or go to the music hall and practice my clarinet. I decided to finish a magazine article with pictures of soldiers in Korea. I was always looking for shots of former members of the Fearless Four. I started to read when I heard a girl's voice.

"Hi."

I looked up at the girl sitting in front of me. "Isn't your name Oscar?"

I was in a slight state of shock. I simply nodded.

"I thought so. My name's Alice. I know your sister Martha."

I got Mayer to excuse both of us. I took her to the music hall, which was empty except for Lloyd Smith practicing his gold trombone in one of the sound-proofed rooms. I fell in love to the sounds of chords and scales from a golden trombone. I had been way down girl-wise ever since Jane Addison told me I stunk. The world simply changed when I looked into those big, innocent green-hazel eyes. The braces on her teeth made mince-meat out of Madeline Hart's horse mouth. The little scar above her upper lip I remember to this day. Even though she walked with a limp because of polio, still she agreed to dance with me at the school dance in the gymnasium after the basketball game.

The following Friday, I met her in the bleachers after the Oakdale Mustangs beat the Tracy Bulldogs. She told me she'd dumped her boyfriend Carl. We had exchanged pictures the day before. We had all had them taken for the *Oracle*, the high school yearbook. I had inscribed, "Words can't express the feelings I have for you . . . Oscar."

While we danced to Freddy Gardner's "I'm In The Mood For

114

Love," she said, "Thanks for the picture . . . I feel the same way."
And that did it. I knew then that she would be forever my *Miss
It*. I froze. I literally could not move. I was paralyzed from head
to toe. I freaked out so bad we had to go sit in my car. I got
right down to it. "Will you marry me?"

"I'm just thirteen, Oscar."

"That doesn't matter."

"It might to my mom."

"I'll go ask her," I said.

"Maybe we ought to wait just a little while. I haven't even
mentioned you. I just broke up with Carl tonight. My stepfather
likes him a whole lot."

"You really feel what you said in the gym?"

"I swear to you I do . . . why would I have gotten rid of
Carl if I didn't?"

"I just want to make sure, 'cause I'm serious."

"Me, too. I would never lie."

"Well . . . maybe we should wait until I meet your folks."

"I think that we should. Daddy's kind of strict. He's a deacon
in the church."

"What are you?"

"Baptist. And you?"

"Sort of a Catholic. I got confirmed."

"But you believe in Jesus, don't you?" she asked with her cute
little scar over her lip bobbing up and down when she spoke.
"You're a Christian?"

"Sure. I told you I was Catholic."

"Daddy says some Catholics don't believe in Jesus."

"You can tell him this one does. He's my favorite saint."

"Saint? He's the son of God, not a saint."

"Oh, that's right. I was thinking of Joseph . . . you know, 'Jesus,
Mary and Joseph, I give you my heart and my soul.' "

"We don't pray that way," she said.

"Well, when we get married, you'll learn all that stuff. Don't
worry, it isn't hard to memorize those prayers. I used to get gold
stars without hardly even trying."

"I wonder what daddy will say about that?"

"He hasn't any choice. The Pope says I can only marry a
Catholic."

"Well . . . we'll cross that bridge when we come to it."

"Yeh, you're right . . . I guess we should make a plan real
soon."

"I'll ask mom if . . . will you take me to the show?"

My heart pounded madly. "God, I'd even take you to meet my grandmother!"

I kissed her mouth and ran my tongue on her braces. To this day nothing makes me go limp as fast as a cripple. Anyone with a brace, a cast or a bandage has me under her spell. Whenever I see a girl with braces, no matter how ugly or fat she may be, I simply get buttery inside the gut. She told me she'd ask her mother that Saturday and let me know the following Monday.

All weekend I couldn't eat. I couldn't drink beer or eat Polish sausages. I thought of my love every single minute for two whole days. My mother tried to get me to lay down and my father gave me one of those strange horsetrader looks he usually did when he suspected I was up to something. Monday finally arrived and I got to school an hour early. She didn't come to school that day . . . an automobile accident? A polio attack? Perhaps she got gored by one of those fucking bulls I've seen in their field. I saw Carl, her ex and asked him if he knew anything. The skinny Okie pretended not to know. I asked Geraldine Watkins, Dragalong's sister. I had her inquire of Marylou, Vernon Knecht's sister and anyone else she could think of. But the only information, my only clue was that she had been to Young People's meeting at the church on Sunday night and then didn't stay for the regular church service.

I arrived home knowing I'd have one hell of a night to go through. I dismissed going to her house because I wasn't sure what a strict Baptist was. In my life there were only Catholics, Protestants and Holy Rollers. Since she was from Oklahoma, I assumed a Baptist was a Holy Roller and to me that meant a wild fanatic who jumped up on pews and screamed to Jesus until he foamed at the mouth. So I figured I'd better wait it out like Bogey had done in *Casablanca*.

When my mother walked into the kitchen with a letter in her hand I immediately knew what had happened. One of those mysteries of life that no man can explain, I knew the jig was up . . . somehow she had found out about my cousin with the itch! I had never before received a letter from a girl, but I knew the contents even before I ripped it open like a con on death row waiting for a word from the governor.

Of course I was wrong. It wasn't a matter of my beastly sex life. It was my family name. When she told her mother the name of her new boyfriend, the old bag said no dice. Never. Forget it. And she was never to speak to me again. In fact, she made her write the letter so that she wouldn't have to explain the situation to me in person.

So goodbye, my love and please don't say hello to me in study-

116

hall. Was that it? What a fool, I thought. There's no problem in a name change. Hell, if she can change her religion, why can't I change my name? I was unaware of my tears when my mother asked me if I was still sick. I asked her what she thought of my changing my name.

"I think Oscar's a nice name," she said.

"No. Not Oscar."

"But you never use your holy name."

"No, ma, I don't mean Thomas either."

She stopped patting the dough for the tortillas and stared me right in the face. "You'll go to hell if you change your family name. And your dad will probably hang you again."

"Geez, you can't take a joke at all, ma. You're getting old."

She must have told the Captain because for three days he called me Thomas, the middle name I'd adopted when I made my confirmation into the Catholic Church. But he never said a word to me about it because he was a horsetrader.

I saw her the next day in study hall and we went to one of the practice rooms together. Alice could cry better than any woman I've known in my life. She made no noise at all. Her eyes didn't get red and no snot ever dripped from her fine nose. Just warm, thick syrup filled the pools of green-hazel and gently spilled over peach skin. She didn't sob, didn't even act as if she were crying. But, God how I felt it. How I was sucked into her existence, her history, her feelings. It was like this: her real father was a drunk. A railroad man living in sin up in Eureka. She loved him. Her mother had married again. The deacon was an American from Arkansas. He tried to rape her when she was twelve. And he hated Mexicans more than life itself. He told her mother that if she permitted Alice to go out with a Mexican he'd divorce her. Period.

Of course that didn't stop us. For Christ sake, we were in love. She was thirteen and I was sixteen. What else is there to say? I could only see her at school. I couldn't telephone her. When I saw them on the street I had to turn or run the other way. But what the hell, *she loved me!* For the time being it was enough.

When the campaign for the Oracle Queen started up, I told Alice to run and I'd manage her. *The Oracle* was our yearbook, and the candidates sold tickets to raise funds. The one with the most tickets became the Queen and was crowned at the dance, the major bash of the winter. I ran my ass ragged in that campaign. The threats upon my life, the assassinations of my character didn't deter me. I pushed those tickets upon everyone in my family, all my friends, and every person I could corner at the Pink Elephant.

117

I worked harder for her election in 1952 than I did for JFK in '60.

She won and was crowned Queen while I sat proud as hell with my face burning in the saxophone section of Mayer's dance band. We played Stan Kenton's *Melody In RFF* while they crowned her. I had not, of course, been able to escort her, because her stepfather had driven her and told her he'd wait until the dance was over to take her home. I alternated between watching my Cinderella and her skinny, pasty-faced rapist stepfather while they put the diamond tiara on her lovely locks.

And then Beverly Learch got even with me for not taking her to the Football Banquet. As the editor of the *Oracle* that year she got to be the master of ceremonies. She gave the usual phony speech and then said, *over the microphone,* "And now if the band will play a waltz, the Queen will be honored with the first dance. . . . Will her escort please step forward?"

The God awful spotlight fell upon me like a seizure by the devil of lightning. The crowd roared with delight. I couldn't move. I couldn't breathe. Suddenly someone rammed a spike into my ass. I jumped up with sweat pouring into my cracked lips. It was Lloyd Smith's golden trombone urging me to go meet my beloved. I gathered all the wisdom my father had taught me. I dug deep into *The Seabee's Manual* for strength. I gritted my teeth and plunged ahead into the roar of the crowd with my legs taut and my face up and my shoulder to the midsection. Fuck it, she is my Queen, I said to myself as I took her hand and carried her around to the Viennese waltz for 10,000 hours while the filthy scum looked at us.

We did not speak during the waltz. When it was over I merely said to her, "Tonight's the night. We'll just have to face it."

"I'm not worried. I know you can handle him," my Queen said.

I rushed her from the roar of the crowd and into my faithful '34 Ford. We said very little as we drove to Riverbank. We waited in the car outside her house for her stepfather to arrive. But two hours later it was Lauren, the Chief of Police, who arrived with *my parents* in the back seat. Judgement day was upon me. Be sure your sins will find you out, the nuns were fond of telling us at catechism. And they sure did that night. They caught us cold. Holding hands in the moonlight while the cows slept.

Alice's parents came out of the house the minute the police

car drove into the driveway behind mine. The stepfather had parked his car in the barn before we arrived. Her mother looked exactly like her, only a bit older. My folks looked like prisoners in Lauren's car. They looked much older, their bodies seemed crippled. Yet I detected a horsetrader smirk under the surface of the humble Indian from the mountains of Durango.

Lauren, the giant Okie in Texas Ranger outfit, walked slowly, carrying the weight of his office in every sigh.

"Evening, Mizz Brown . . . I brought his folks . . ."

No one volunteered a sound.

"Oscar? . . ." The Texas Ranger was having difficulty. I held the wheel tightly. The young girl was dead for all practical purposes.

"Now, it's this way . . . Alice's folks here? . . . They done called me." He just couldn't get up steam. "Now I don't like to poke my nose into *private* matters . . . you understand that?"

"Why'd you bring my parents into this?" I spoke up.

"I *wanted* to come, son," my old man said. "He was checking the place when he got the call."

"Now, Oscar, like I was saying . . . Mr. and Mrs. Brown here. They already done signed a *complaint* so it ain't exactly *private* no more. I got nothing to say about it no more . . . if I catch you two together again . . . I'll just have to take you both into juvenile . . . it's already been done . . . now, I known you for . . . since you was just a tyke . . . but under the law, if I catch you, I'll take you in . . . Savvy?" He tried to smile.

Perhaps if he hadn't thrown in that "savvy" bit I'd have kept still, but as it stood, I lashed out: *"Chinga tu madre, cabron!"*

He whipped around to my old man. "I done tried, Man-u-el. Now you just take him from here."

Without another word my folks got into the car. Alice was still frozen. "I'll see you later, babe," I said to her.

"Did you hear that, chief?" the scurvy Arkie said.

"Oh, why don't you shut up!" my old mother said.

"Now, Jennie . . ." the Chief began.

"My wife's name is Mrs. Acosta," the Captain said.

"Let's go, dad." I leaned into Alice and helped her out.

We drove away, back to the West Side. The only thing my folks said was, "She sure is a *pretty* girl." I began to laugh before we got home. I kept laughing as we walked into the bar, which was closed. My old man got us each a beer without a word. I was caught up in uncontrollable laughter. The convulsions down under began on that night. The wretched vomit, the gas laden belly formed within my pit when the chief of police asked me if I understood. Savvy?

I hear Dr. Serbin say, "You still insist on blaming your troubles on Alice's father?"

I looked up and saw him sitting on top of Mr. Hemingway's grave. The sun had nearly set now and the cottonwoods were giving up their summer snow.

The Owl approaches from my rear. "Ah, you're both full of bullshit . . . Osc here ain't never had no problems. He just needs to get his shit together."

I left them both arguing at the grave. They no longer mattered to me. I drove back to town to load up on Budweiser. Coming out of the country store I ran into Karin. She carried a giant-sized bag of potato chips and a whole box of ten-cent packages of Koolaid.

"Henry Hawk!" she shouted.

She gave me the directions to her place and I promised to drop by for a beer.

"We're having guacamole," she said as she drove away in her bronze Porsche.

Chapter Ten

I'm still on the run as I enter the Wilmington spread beside a creek at the foot of a huge expanse of evergreens rising to catch an ascending moon. I am introduced to young men with long hair just two inches below the ear lobes. They sit stiffly in pressed jeans and I forget their names immediately. Karin is into floor-length printed flowers swishing for one guest to another. A thin-lipped kid with dandruff enters the porch where we are sitting, lightly tasting German beer. I have heard sounds and seen moving lips, but so far nothing has happened. My green Plymouth sits outside the mansion ready to roll.

"Hey, sis, anymore beer?" the kid asks.

"Gee, Phare, I guess not. Isn't there any wine in the cellar?"

"Fuck! A fine party this is!" he pouts and returns to the house.

A fine party, indeed! Here I am, forced to share my beer with blond-haired strangers who don't speak my language. Perhaps the old man is saving for the next potato season. Could it be they don't drink? I have known people who don't talk, but only after the bozo has got to them. What the hell do they teach them in the potato patch anyway? Maybe that's why the rich chick split for Acapulco. But she was hitchhiking. I myself only seek hand-outs when I am down. Surely they have money. Look at that furniture, and classy house and the brand new sports cars parked next to your filthy, green Plymouth. Greedy? Stingy?

"Karin," I weakly call to her. She flits over as if I had *demanded* her presence. Her entire attention is upon me. I am the most important person in the whole wide world. "Say, do you want me to go and get some beer?"

"Heavens no! The goodies will be here shortly. Michael is bringing *the dip*. Be patient, my friend." Languid, blue eyes and a perfect bust, that's my style. This is real class. If only they'd come to life. She *must* want me. Didn't she drink beer and listen to my life story for ten hours? Didn't she insist I call her? Like she says, hold tight, soon I'll have her at the creek. When these creeps finish their beer and swallow the famous dip, then you'll be together. Alone in the moonlight. Obviously she doesn't know you're a brown buffalo. Maybe the beach boys in Acapulco were not quite enough. She must go for you Latin types, else why would she go through all this trouble?

A short, hard-faced woman enters. Lipstick and powder. She wears a pink negligee. Firm breasts and a tight ass make up for the rest. She carries a quart-sized bowl in cellophane. Everyone stands and we follow her into the black yard. The moon is full. Cool breeze blows down from the massive black sheets of mountains at our fingertips. A man with a mustache and a pipe in his mouth walks right behind her with several forks and a thirty-nine-cent bag of Fritos. People stand around and gawk at the bowl on the picnic table. There's a murmur in the crowd. A tenseness. They eye the bowl as if it were some God damn snake! Now Karin comes out with a fucking gallon of Koolaid. And the cast is complete when her brother, the kid with the thin lips, brings a stack of paper cups. It is a night to howl! The fucking Fourth of July, do you understand? No time for music or any bullshit, partner. Avocados and Koolaid, motherfucker! This is Sun Valley, Idaho. John Fitzgerald Kennedy slept here. Jackie got raped by a bear up in that mountain. Do I make myself clear? Do you get the picture?

The woman with the lipstick pushes her way to the center. The bridegroom at her side is going to help her cut the cake.

She has the voice of a drowning frog. "Karin, Michael sent this over. He had to leave for Alpine. A bunch of mothers from Chicago came in to see him. Will you do us the honors?"

The princess from Acapulco waltzes to the stage. The man with the pipe assists her. He rips open the Frito bag. She dips in and lifts the magic potion to her lovely lips. She swallows and her eyes close. For seven seconds we wait in silence. Will she turn into an owl, an egg or a flamenco dancer? I can hear the sparks from the bonfire spitting up flames. A huge smile forms about her face. "Perfect. Simply perfect." And without more ado, the crowd decends upon the bowl.

"Don't you want to try it?" the woman with the negligee asks.

"I'm not hungry," I say.

"You don't have to stuff yourself."

"I'm not into Koolaid anymore," I explain to the hard-nosed bitch.

"Oh, but it's spiked. You really should try it. By the way, I'm Gerri."

"Howdy." I take her hand and she feels the inside of my palm with her two longest fingers. Holy Jesus, in Riverbank that meant you wanted to fuck! I must restrain myself. After all, this is potato country.

"I'll bet you're an Aries?"

"Not really. I'm Samoan."

Gerri got a laugh out of that one. Am I getting drunk by osmosis, I thought. She continued to hold my hand. My face began to burn. It must be the hot air coming in through the window. Nevada was a drag.

"Karin said you're a friend of Turk?"

"I'm his lawyer," I said.

"Really?"

"Want to see my bar card?"

"She said you're just passing through?"

"She told me I was dropping out . . . Say, look, uh . . . are you finished reading my palm?"

"Sorry 'bout that. One tends to forget things with this peyote."

"*That's* what you've got in the guacamole?"

"Is that the way you pronounce it?" the woman with the frog voice said.

"We do in Samoa."

She laughed again. A hard laugh that reminded me of Maria in Trader JJ's. She slapped me on the shoulder. "Hey man, *I like you*. What's your name?"

"They call me Henry Hawk."

"Nice to know you." She reached for my hand.

"You've already read my chart."

"Oh, that's right . . . don't you like peyote?"

"Is it anything like mayonnaise?"

"Henry Hawk! You come with me. Mother Gerri is going to teach you something new." She grabbed my hand and hauled me over to the picnic table. She scooped up a slab of the spread in a Frito chip and shoved it in my mouth. Foul scum, green turd with arsenic is what it tasted like. But I am a man, a macho who eats hot chili for a penny a bite, remember?

"I take it you didn't go to Acapulco with Karin?" I politely inquire.

"Someone had to keep the shop open. Why, don't you like it?"

"You can't be serious. It tastes horrible. Jesus!"

"Oh, but it isn't supposed to taste good. Don't you really know what peyote is?"

"Well, shit, I assume it's some kind of a fucking narcotic."

" 'Narcotic' he says! Wow, you really are a lawyer, aren't you, Henry Hawk?"

"I have only one client. John Tibeau," I call out. We watch the moon high up the mountainside for five minutes. "Yes, John Tibeau is my only client."

"That's the spirit. Here, try it one more time. Let mother help you." Once again the green death comes into my mouth and the sparks from the flame rip into the sky. "Now wash it down with this nice baby punch."

"This sure beats Budweiser," I am telling my mother while she cleans out my ears with Koolaid. The others have changed into their Fourth of July costumes. Phare has a bandage over his forehead and is playing a snare drum. Karin sits on top of the table, next to the peyote, with her legs crossed in yoga. She is sewing Frito chips on the American flag. One chip for each state. The moon has fallen into the bonfire and cannons are exploding behind the trees. All the boys and girls have left the party. We are in the battlefield waiting for the British with sparklers and firecrackers up our noses. Gerri is desperately trying to stuff a cherry bomb in my ear. "It's too fucking small, Samoa man. I can't get it in!"

I jump up and push her aside. "Don't you dare fuck with my ears, woman. I don't give a damn if it is the Fourth of July."

She stands and holds me tight. "I'm sorry. You were telling me your mother never breast fed you. You *asked* me to put a bomb in your ear, you bastard!"

Before we can finish our discussion, a straight woman enters the show. She stands tall. Upright, and one that escheweth all evil. The party comes to a grinding halt. It is mums. Karin casts aside her flag and pulls her dress down to her knees. "Listen everybody. I want you all to meet mums. She is my daddy's wife."

The tall woman speaks. "I am your daddy's mistress, wicked girl."

Everyone gets a big bang out of that one. The kid with the snare drum runs up to the tall woman and kisses her smack in the lips. "This is my mother, gang . . . now, mommy, we'd like you to try something that your daughter brought back to us from Acapulco."

Karin butts in. "I did not. I got it from this man who gave me a ride. There he is, mums." She points at me. I remove my hand from Gerri's earlobes. "He's from the islands. Turk Tibeau sent it with him," she screams.

"I am his lawyer. I represent Mr. Tibeau. Pleased to meet you, madam."

The tall woman cannot see through the flames. She daintily takes a Frito chip and plunges it into the bowl. Everyone immediately removes his costume while the straight woman stuffs the guacamole between her ruby lips. They all snicker and giggle and guffaw because they've snagged another fish.

"Beautiful, my dear. It's lovely. From the islands, you say?" Again she scoops up a batch. She smacks her lips and licks her teeth. "Delightful. Simply delightful." Her son hands her a cup of the Koolaid. She washes it down with a flare. "And what'd you say it was? Guacamole?"

"Yes, mums. From Samoa."

"Oh, not from Acapulco?"

"They've cleaned up Acapulco," I say to them. "You can only get this kind of avocado in the San Blas Islands."

"What a pity," she tsk-tsks her royal head.

All the others have their eyes ready for her reaction. They are waiting—praying—for her to get the ghost.

"She'll never know what hit her," Gerri giggles in my ear.

"This stuff is supposed to *do* something to you?" the Samoan says.

125

"Why do you think she's licking the bowl with her fingers?"

"Because she's got class. It isn't polite to lick it with your tongue."

She turns and goes into the fire. Mrs. Wilmington waltzes to my side. She is at least a foot taller than I. "Isn't that avocado simply wonderful?"

"Has it hit you yet?" I inquire.

"Not yet. I've been drinking cognac," she says. I look up into her Greek face and say to the goddess, "It will."

She winks at me. "I know. I wasn't born yesterday, you know."

When Gerri returns I tell her that the trick didn't work. "It turned her on, didn't it?"

"Yeh, but she knew it was a drug."

"So what? Everyone knows it's a drug."

But the fireworks started up again. Huge blasts of red, white and blue light up the skies. Bombs explode and rockets soar. Phare brings out the stereo and plays Cream. He tells me he is a serious musician and I tell him about my stint with the Air Force Band.

When I finished puking for the tenth time, I find myself behind a tree, my head in Gerri's lap. "Ulcers. Just my ulcers. I create art with the insides of my belly. My puke is a new art form," I explain.

"Listen, Mr. Samoa man . . . I know you are on a search," my mother says.

"Search, your ass. I'm just looking for a good doctor."

"That's what I mean . . . now when you leave here, go to Alpine. It's on the way. A friend of Tibeau's lives there. Go to a bar called the Daisy Duck and ask the bartender for Bobby Miller. He'll tell you where to go from there. Bobby knows a lot of good doctors that specialize in ulcers. Just tell him that Mother Gerri sent you."

Sometime later, I don't know when, I found myself asleep in my green sleeping bag beside a creek. I'll never know how I found my way to the site of Ernest Hemingway's statue near the ski lift in Sun Valley. But it didn't matter. I was alone in the dark beside the rushing water and the pain in my stomach was easing with the avocado mix. I stared at the stars and thought of old Ernie and his corny stories about the Left Bank and all the fine wines and wonderful meals he guzzled with his lesbian friends. I couldn't understand why he had to go all the way to Paris to look for companionship when Karin and Gerri were just around the corner from his house in Ketchum, Idaho. Maybe he just couldn't take it, I thought to myself as I fell asleep.

126

With the sun at ten o'clock high, I was awakened by the sounds of children walking through the woods. They were tourists in search of the statue where I lay. I jumped up, grabbed my sleeping bag and soon I was behind the wheel of my green Plymouth in search of Bobby Miller and the Daisy Duck.

Chapter Eleven

After Lauren threatened us with jail, Alice and I went underground. The last six months of my senior year at Oakdale Joint I only saw her during school hours. On special occasions, like the Junior-Senior Prom, I'd get Bob Whitt to pick her up for me and pretend he was her date. But after a couple of times he refused to do it anymore because her old man wanted to know if he had serious intentions of getting married.

"That Okie sonofabitch even asked me what church I belonged to," my penguin-nosed friend said.

After that, we just gave up. We made the decision to simply suffer. The day she was eighteen—four years hence—we'd get married in my mother's Catholic church. Then the two of us would conquer the world alone.

So a few weeks after I graduated, I joined the U.S. Air Force because they promised to place me in a marching band. I figured the best thing to do was to stay away from Riverbank until our wedding, and the four-year enlistment was just the thing to do.

But it didn't work very well. That very month the Air Force had opened up a new training station in Pleasanton, California. Park's Air Force Base was located exactly fifty-five miles from Riverbank and I started going home on weekends to meet Alice in dark alleys or at the home of some friend.

After several months of basic training and band school, they sent me all the way to Hamilton Air Force Base in Marin County, about 120 miles from Riverbank. It seemed we were destined to be together. I begged to go to Korea but they told me I had to follow orders, stay near San Francisco and play my clarinet for the returning heroes.

Then one day I got a dear john letter from *Miss It*. She said she just couldn't stand to lie to her mother anymore. That it was too dangerous. God would punish her. And her stepfather would divorce her mother if he found out we were still seeing each other.

Since I'd joined the Air Force just because of her, I saw no reason for continuing the tragedy. I asked my C.O. if there was any way I could get an immediate discharge. After he kicked me out of his office, I decided to go AWOL.

I hitch-hiked to San Francisco and stayed drunk for three days. I walked into 100 bars looking for a beautiful broad only to wind up in the Fillmore District in some stinking joint filled with junkies. I got into an argument with a baldheaded nigger and he pulled a switchblade. I was crowded against the wall. I pointed my index finger in the pocket of my Air Force, shade #76, blue rain coat, looked him straight in the eye and said, "Now you just put that down real slowly before I blow your balls off."

I got back to the base a day late and told my C.O. that I'd been given a mickey finn and couldn't wake up until Monday.

So instead of running away, I decided to become a serious musician. I'd drink every night at the base cafeteria, then sit on a park bench and cry for my beloved. A couple of blocks down the jet planes carried bombs to fight the communist hordes in Korea.

Three months later I got a letter from Alice saying she'd gotten married to an old friend of ours, the left tackle on the Oakdale Mustangs who'd once told me he'd love to eat her snatch. He was darker skinned than me, an Italian with a heavy beard and a Catholic; so I figured her stepfather was just down on Mexicans, period. She ended the seven-page letter with an appeal for me to turn to God, to ask his forgiveness for everything we'd done.

Even though I never screwed her, I went to confession for the first time in five years and told the priest that I had committed a mortal sin.

"What have you done, my son?" the voice from behind the black veil spoke.

"I've made a . . . god out of my girlfriend."

"How?"

"I don't understand it, father. But when I say my prayers, I see her sitting on the altar. She's one of those false gods the sisters told me about."

He told me it was perfectly normal, that I shouldn't worry. He asked me to say ten Our Father's and seven Hail Mary's and all would be forgiven.

I did the penance but there were no miracles. I still felt guilty as sin for worshipping Alice, especially after she'd dumped me for a greasy, God damn Wop. So I started to read the Bible and go to church every night. One of the guys in the band, a redheaded trombone player from Pomona who read philosophy started to tell me about his religion. He was a Baptist and gave me endless leaflets explaining all I had to do to be saved. He insisted that I leave the Roman Catholic Church immediately, because it was the "house of the Anti-Christ" prophesied by St. John the Divine in the *Book of Revelations.*

After a month of reading, I knew at least enough to argue. I tried to prove to him why the Catholic Church was *not* the Church on Seven Hills referred to by St. John. He laughed at my fertile explanations and said, "How about Purgatory. Where's that in the Bible?" When I couldn't come up with a rational explanation, I went and talked to a scholar-priest who taught at a high school near the base. He showed me a single sentence in the Old Testament where King David mentioned that his dead son was neither in heaven nor in hell . . . "Ergo, there must be an intermediate place," he said tugging on his pipe. I couldn't believe a word he said.

I finally gave up on Catholicism and admitted to Duane Dunham that he knew more about Jesus than I did. We went into the boiler room under the barracks and he called down the Holy Ghost to save me. I took Jesus as my savior and became a Baptist right on the spot.

I talked Jesus morning, noon and night. I was a fanatic of the worst kind. During band rehearsals, in the chow line, late at night in the barracks while lonely kids wrote letters to their sweethearts. I preached instant salvation to the jazz musicians of the band.

Within three months I was holding noon-time prayer meetings in the boiler room for about a dozen of the boys in the band. I got elected president of the Young People's Club at the Petaluma

Baptist Church because I could testify to more sin and corruption than these egg farmers had ever dreamed existed. I told them of sins I'd never even tried. And they ate it all up and made me their hero.

I got so good at it, I even converted my entire family, with the exception of my brother Bob, who decided to stay with the Pope. My old man had never had any formal religion, so he agreed with every word I told him. My ma saw how Jesus had cleaned me up, so it seemed like a good idea. They got saved while I was on a three day pass and sold the Pink Elephant bar the following month. They never drank again and lived happily ever after. But of course they screwed up my three sisters with Jesus as a Baptist, morning, noon and night.

Then the Air Force sent me to Panama. I played clarinet with the Fighting 573rd Air Force Marching and Dance Band at Hamilton Air Force Base, which had the highest V.D. rate of any base in the world in June of 1954.

My very first weekend I went into Balboa, the American sector of the Panama Canal Zone, and joined the First Southern Baptist Church. With my credentials as a former president of the Young People's Club and my exotic ancestry, I was an instant hit. The short little man with the Hitler mustache grabbed my hand and pumped the shit out of it and said, "Do you know Jesus?"

I told Pastor Beebee I knew Him well and asked him if he could set me up as a missionary. He saw me coming and took me under his wings. He gave me a panel truck with the sides cut out and seats in the back, a portable pump organ and all the literature I could use. Then he pointed me in the direction of the jungle where the heathens lived.

Before it was over, I had built a mission in Chilibre, a small village with black Jamaicans and brown Panamanians, and one at the Palo Seco Leper Colony. They had been waiting for someone like me all their life. We built a church out of palm trees and mango leaves. We sang in Spanish and in English and occasionally I played my clarinet for them and warned them against civilization. I told them to stay out of Panama City, to lay off their home brew made from masticated corn and to quit smoking coco leaves. In return, I no longer went to movies, quit playing jazz and didn't touch my penis except to piss for two whole years.

They elected me to the Board of Deacons at the First Baptist Church in Balboa after I became so successful in the jungle. They even sent some of my color slides to the churches back home and told them that a "Mexican Billy Graham" was converting natives right and left. In exchange the Southern Baptists sent Pastor Beebee more money to make new additions to the church. It already looked like an old mansion on a southern plantation.

But I never got invited to the home of any church member. I had no social life except in the jungle where the wild orchids grew and the land crabs scattered at the sound of my feet trampling through the foliage in search of more natives to tell about Jesus.

The guys in the band tempted me. They wanted to see me fall from grace. They offered me women, cigarettes and beer. They invited me to parties. They even brought skinny-legged girls with their boobs hanging out to invite me to their homes. And the more they tried, the more I prayed. I took to rising at 3:00 A.M. to pray and read my Bible. I had every afternoon, evening and weekend to do my missionary work. I'd told the leader of the dance band that jazz was against my religion; so for the next two years I had afternoons, evenings, and weekends free to save souls.

But I was miserable. I hurt inside. I didn't have the peace of mind that Jesus promised if we did his work. I didn't have the very thing I preached. Finally, in January of 1956 when I had but six months to go on my tour of duty, I made up my mind to settle it once and for all. I made a final study of the Bible and wrote down everything that sounded true in a notebook on my right. Those things that sounded wrong or inconsistent or that I couldn't believe, I wrote in a notebook to my left. For three months, between 3:00 and 7:00 A.M., sitting under a single bulb in the attic above the barracks, I made a comparative study of the Synoptic Gospels.

When I finished, the left-handed notebook was completely filled with chapter and verse and reasons why I could not believe in Christianity. The right-handed notebook contained about two pages of homilies on love.

So I gave up Jesus and the Baptist Church. But I still had three months to go. How could I now go to all my congregations with the San Blas Indians (whom I was also teaching English), the black Jamaicans, and the brown Panamanians and after two years of preaching Christ suddenly tell them I thought it was all a crock of shit? I couldn't. Instead, I just continued to preach sermons on love and peace and goodwill toward man, etc.

I despised myself for being a hypocrite, but it seemed the right thing to do. It was better that I suffer than that I should now totally confuse the minds of those whom I'd taught and loved for two years. I never breathed a word about my final study to anyone during those last few months.

In June of 1956 they flew me back to the States, gave me an honorable discharge and $8000. I ended up in New Orleans where I got drunk, smoked cigarettes and cursed God for the first time in two years. I was reeling drunk in a little green room at the St. Regis Hotel not far from the French Quarter when I finally took it upon myself to end the pain and sorrow. I opened the window, looked down at the cars parked behind the hotel some ten stories down and decided to jump. I knew I had on clean underwear, the money was in the safe of the hotel and my discharge papers with my home address were on the chest of drawers. Ma would get the money.

I was twenty-one and without God. I had no one to love me and no one for me to love. Since there was no after-life, what then did it matter?

I leaned forward, ready to lurch to my doom when I thought, "Jesus, but it's going to hurt when I hit those bumpers!"

Suddenly I hear the voice of Dr. Serbin, "But of course, you didn't go through with it?"

I look up to find myself deep in the Rockies. I hear the garbled voice of the Owl. "He ain't got the balls to do himself in."

"Ah, fuck off, you lousy bums. What do you know about death?" I scream at my two head-hunters as I tear open another Bud and roar down the road towards salvation at the Daisy Duck.

Chapter Twelve

The next day, I arrived in Alpine battered by the winds of my misfortune, caught in the toils of my rejections and battered by that illness of self-pity so common to drunken Indians gone amok. But I did not blame myself. My tormentors were legion. Who was I to accuse? And why should I take the rap? After all, I had made my confirmation and graduated from high school. I had heard the call of Jesus and received the Holy Spirit without rebellion. And didn't I go beyond my mother's wildest dreams? Was I not in fact a lawyer, and did I not counsel the poor and the needy until my very own red blood poured from my mouth? What fault was it of mine that my secretary died of cancer or that the doctor had no cure for my ulcers? No, it was through no fault of mine that I rejected the rewards this society had for men such as myself. I *had* minded my p's and q's and I had committed *The Seabee's Manual* to heart. What else in God's name could they expect of me?

I slept for twenty-four hours at the Log Cabin Motel. I awoke when it was dark to find myself in a small, western town, high in the Rockies. With fifty dollars to my name I went out in search of the Daisy Duck and the man who would show me the way to salvation.

I asked the perch-faced, bearded bartender if he knew Bobby Miller. The bar was empty. My man was not around. But if I waited, his girl friend would be there soon. I took my beer to the deck. Through the darkness of the night I could see a gigantic sheet of mountain right behind us, perfect for an avalanche into the rear door of the bar. The moon was still full and the trees stood guard amongst the pin-points of lights high above. The stars were falling but I had nowhere to hide. Fifty dollars wouldn't get me back to Serbin's couch or Trader JJ's pool table.

I heard high-heeled footsteps on the wooden planks of the sun deck. "Are you looking for Miller?" a light wind called out.

She wore purple tights under a pink mini-dress. A short girl with short brown hair and sensible breasts. I told her about Gerri, Wilmington and Tibeau. She seemed pleased to greet me and invited me in for a drink. Things were looking up. Her ass held firm as she swayed in her white, high heeled shoes. When she told me her name was Bobbi, I wondered if perhaps Gerri hadn't misread my palm. I was certain from the way this girl talked as she leaned her white arms on the bar at my elbow that *she* could save me from *whatever* ailed me. She introduced me to the bartender and told him I was a friend of Tibeau.

"Oh, yeh? What's that freak up to now?" Phil, the bartender, honked with gravel between his teeth.

"I haven't seen him for months. Actually, I'm a friend of his brother's," I lied.

"I don't blame you," he threw it back at me.

Bobbi went about her business while I talked with Phil. She was the cocktail waitress. I kept looking at her from the side. Soon she came up and said, "Hey, man, why don't we dance?"

I had never been asked to dance by a stranger. I am not the sort of person people approach. Perhaps it's my bearing. They say I scowl, that I'm over zealous, threatening in appearance. I call immediate attention to myself. Yet when I speak my voice is soft, medium in tone and, unless I'm pissed, pleasant to hear. But girls and women never, ever speak to me first. Yet this lovely little chick led me by the hand and swung me around the floor to "White Rabbit." And me with my construction boots and cut-up Arrow shirt!

When we returned to the bar two men were talking with

Phil. Bobbi introduced me to a short, stocky kid with fat boots and a kind face. There was a gentleness in Miller's green eyes, a calmness in his voice that immediately disarmed me. I gave him back his chick and never again had dirty thoughts about her. The other one was tall and on the verge of losing his hair. He wore short pants, an upside-down sailor's cap from L.L. Bean and a holstered knife hung from his waist. He looked the other way when Bobbi introduced me to Miller and told him I'd been in Ketchum.

"This is King," Miller said. "He's a friend of Turk's."

Christ, I thought, another bike rider from Chicago! He turned, gave me a quick once-over and said, "You from San Francisco, too?"

"Nah, I'm from Riverbank."

"I thought Turk was in San Francisco," the short one said.

"He was the last time I saw him. Still riding his bike."

"Riding his bike? I thought the sonofabitch had a full cast. Isn't his leg broken?" King's voice was on edge. He spoke rapidly. He wanted quick information.

"It was. But somehow he manages to ride."

The tall one turned to Miller. "You know, I'll bet that bastard was lying to me. From his letter, I thought he was all fucked up."

"Oh, don't worry, King. Turk's not going to sue you. He was just kidding, I'll bet," Bobbi said to calm the man down.

"I'm not worried about that. He's too strung out to even *think* about getting a lawyer. But he keeps writing me these long, wretched letters trying to make me feel guilty."

"If you're talking about his accident, he *did* go see a lawyer," I said.

"Oh, he did, hey? So *that's* his action." His eyes narrowed and his balding head nodded. "He's going to play *that* game now."

"King was driving the bike when Tibeau broke his leg," Miller said to me.

"I know." Now I remembered the freak of whom John had spoken. John Tibeau had that great fault—to those of us at JJ's—of talking to us of *Great-Men-I-Have-Known*. He kept constantly on the run between New York and San Francisco, crashing every party given by *famous people* in order to take the good news to the other end of the table. He pestered us with names and titles and associations. But he did it well. And so, when he showed me an autographed copy of King's book and asked me to buy him a beer while I thumbed through it, the devil was setting me up for this confrontation with the tall, baldheaded hillbilly from Tennessee.

"Tibeau told me all about the accident," I said to him.

"Is he serious about suing me?"

"I haven't filed the complaint. But if the insurance doesn't cover the medicals . . ."

"*You* haven't? What's your interest in this?" He was clearly agitated. He motioned to Phil with his index finger to serve the four of us.

"None, really. I advised him against suing you. He assumed the risk when he let you drive his bike knowing you were plastered."

Miller asked, "Are you a lawyer, Oscar?"

"I was until a few days ago."

"You mean you were disbarred?" the hillbilly smiled.

"Well . . . I hung it up."

"Then you were just putting me on?"

"About what?"

"I mean, you don't have any Goddamn subpoena for me or anything like that?"

"Jesus, King you're sure paranoid," Miller cut in.

"Well, Christ, how do I know? Guy walks in and tells me he's Turk's lawyer . . . from Riverbank, you say?"

I sipped my beer and let it hang for a moment. "You weren't listening. I don't represent Tibeau. I just gave him some advice."

"Where in the hell is Riverbank. Isn't that down by L.A.?"

"Nah, it's close to Oakdale."

"What's Tibeau doing down there?"

"Like I said, man, you're not listening. I didn't say *Tibeau* was down in Riverbank."

"Yeh, King, he said *he* was from Riverbank," Miller explained.

"Jesus, somebody's got their head twisted here. And you, you fucker," he shouted at the bartender, "let us have some more whiskey here!"

I switched to scotch and we were silent for a minute. I warmed up and started in again. "Tibeau said you were a Hell's Angel."

"I hung up *my* license, too."

"You mean they booted you out," Miller said.

"Are you a *professional* writer?" I asked.

"You got it all wrong, Oscar," Miller said, "King's a farmer. He raises Dobermans. Didn't you see the jacket of his book?"

"No, I don't read too much."

"You probably couldn't get it in Riverbank. The book's in English," the hillbilly said.

"Say, tell me," I said, "do the Hell's Angels *really* carry chains and bullwhips?"

"When they're out on a rumble they do," he said.

"Is that what you and Turk were doing when he busted his leg?"

King gave me a thin-lipped smile and looked me straight in the eye. "No . . . we were out looking for greasers."

"I take it you didn't find any."

Miller said, "Hell, they wouldn't know what to do with them if they did find any. King would probably just interview them while they cut his balls off."

"Yeh," he nodded, "I probably would, if I had an interpreter."

"Then you really are a *professional* writer?" I asked.

"He's just a hack," Miller said.

"Oh, come on you guys," Bobbi said, "I think King's a *good* writer."

We all laughed. "Go ahead and laugh, you bastards! I guess I'm about as much a writer as you are a lawyer," he said to me.

The three of them laughed at me. Miller changed sides with a smile. "Hey, man. I've heard of *shyster* lawyers, but what's a *Mexican* lawyer do?"

"They slide into court on their grease," King said with a straight face.

"Grease?" Bobbi asked. "What are you guys *talking* about?"

"Yeh. Grease. That's what Mexicans use to cook gringos," I said.

"Boy you guys are really something else," Bobbi said.

"They got lot of gringos in Riverbank, Oscar?" Miller asked.

"They used to. I haven't been there in fifteen years."

"I'll bet the town's just full of Mexicans now the way those bastards multiply," the King said.

"Have you been there, King?" Miller asked.

"We don't allow hillbillies on motorcycles," I said.

"They've just got dirt roads for their burros there," the King said.

"And lots of restaurants," I said.

"Why's that?" Miller assisted.

"In case we catch a gringo . . . we like to eat them while the blood's still warm," I said.

"You Aztecs still practice those native rites?" the King asked.

"Are you an *Aztec*?" Bobbi asked.

"For Christ sake, Bobbi, just look at him," Miller said.

The young chick observed my entire body. "Oh, you're putting me on. He doesn't look like an Aztec."

"Sure I do," I protested. "Take a good look."

"I thought they were all dead," she said.

139

"I'm the last one. My family's the last of the Aztecs."

"I don't believe you," she said. "Besides, I thought you said you were a Mexican."

"No, he said he was a fry cook," the King said.

"Oh, you guys are getting smashed!" She got up and went to wait on several customers that had walked in.

We began to down the drinks with the bravado of men in a race, a challenge for the cup, a penny for each spoonful of chili. The hour was drawing near. The music blared rock and roll as we continued.

King asked me, "You just passing through? Or what?"

"Probably just the weekend. I'm waiting for a telegram."

"You don't by any chance know a lawyer named Pierce, do you? He's a friend of Tibeau's. From Richmond."

"I'm not sure. Tibeau brought some famous people in, but I don't know."

"He's the ex-mayor of Richmond," Miller said.

"He's about our age," the King said. "He dropped out, too."

"The last I heard he was on his way to Tibet," Miller said.

"He's going to be a monk," the King added.

"Oh, fuck, I can't take anymore of this!" King stood up and swallowed his drink. "Well, just see to it you're out of town by Monday morning. I'll see you freaks later."

He scrambled out the door and left me alone with Miller.

"He's a pretty good dude," Miller said. "He's just paranoid because all his friends come by here and get all fucked up when they're on the run. He says it interferes with his writing."

"Yeh, he seemed okay to me. Looks like he's on speed."

"God, is he. . . . By the way, are you into any dope?"

"Gerri gave me some peyote a couple of days ago. I'm mainly a boozer."

"She's pretty cool. Listen man, you got a place to stay?"

"I'm paid up for tonight at a motel near by."

"Well, look, if you're going to spend the weekend, why don't you crash at my pad?"

"Thanks, but I don't like to, you know."

"Fuck that shit, man. I can see you're on the run. We have an extra bedroom. It's cool there. Right next to the creek, by the bridge. Just ask anyone. This is a small town. Why don't you come on down tomorrow. Or stay with us tonight."

"Thanks, I guess I don't hide it too well."

"Yeh, man. And Bobbi digs you. She told me to ask you if you wanted to crash over the pad."

140

"I'll drop by tomorrow afternoon if you're going to be there."

"Sure. I've got no plans. I'll turn you on to some hash. A friend of mine just got back from India and left me a piece. In fact he'll probably be there tomorrow. You'll like the guy. He's a pilot. He made some trips for the CIA."

"Jesus Christ!"

"No, man, the dude's cool. He was just on the trip to raise bread so he could smuggle in some good hash. You'll dig the guy."

I said goodnight to him and his chick and walked back to the Log Cabin Motel in the moonlight. I heard owls calling to one another from the aspen trees amongst the cottonwoods as I held tightly to myself and wondered where it would all end up. I was thirty-three years old. I had forty dollars left and I had no idea where I was . . .

Chapter Thirteen

After my honorable discharge from the United States Air Force in June in 1956 and the aborted suicide in New Orleans, I returned to Riverbank to live with my parents. None of my old girlfriends from high school remembered me when I called them. My old drinking buddies disappeared behind the grey walls of various county jails or prisons, so I moved out and enrolled at Modesto Jr. College to study French and creative writing.

My brother Bob, always a year or two ahead of me, had been discharged from the Coast Guard while I was still with the fighting 573rd Air Force Band in Panama. We had retained our joint savings account during our hitch with Uncle Sam in case either of us got killed fighting off the yellow horde in Korea. As it turned out neither of us got within 5,000 miles of a communist, and so I expected to return to a nice little sockful protected by Mr. Wilkie's automatic lock at the Riverbank Farmers Bank. I threatened to sue him when he explained that under the terms of our account my brother had the power to draw out my allotment checks the day they were received and that he had done so. He had been considerate enough to leave twenty-seven dollars for a good drunk, so I couldn't be that mad at him. In any event, he had left for San Francisco the previous semester to study law at Hastings College, so there wasn't much I could do about it.

I could see the poetic justice in his *stealing* the money to go to law school. Besides, now that the war was over, it was time that the Acostas showed their true potential. We could use a lawyer in the family. I completely forgave him when a friend of his I met in my French class told me Bob had ambitions to go into politics. This guy's name was Norman Eudy, and he had the air of a true intellectual: bald, stocky and red in the face. He dabbled in Spanish, German, Italian, French and to my great surprise he was fluent in Okie with an Oxford twang. He had been born in Norman, Oklahoma, but he read Sartre, Dostoyevski and Kierkegaard with a passion and he found it absolutely essential that I understand the relationship between Lefty Frizel and the existential philosophers. You wouldn't be able to understand Norman Eudy. I certainly couldn't, so I found another ex-Okie to do it for me.

Charlie Johnston insisted on the pronounciation of the "t" in his name. "We wouldn't of put it in if we didn't want it pronounced, stupid!" Charlie had signed up for French just to prove to Eudy that an ex-Okie from Blueberry Hill, Oklahoma could get a better grade than an intellectual from Norman. Charlie was tall and skinny. He had black hair, rotten teeth and black-rimmed fingernails. His only saving grace, for my money, was that he played a mean banjo and could actually understand Norman Eudy's interpretations of the *Book of Genesis*. I was just getting over the horrible trauma of four years with the Air Force Band, so I merely tried to listen while we drank buckets of beer at Cheto Connetto's South Seas Pizza House on McHenry between Modesto and Riverbank, the hang-out for all the returned veterans enrolled at the J.C. and the busty, red-cheeked girls from the telephone company.

They introduced me to Cheto as "Bob's brother," the only name I was known by all through high school and likewise now at the small, two-year college for middle-class Okies and farmers' daughters from the San Joaquin Valley. Cheto gave me a limp hand with a twinkle in his small green eyes. I immediately noticed the short distance between the left and the right eye and the waves of his greying hair, carefully arranged to make him look ready for the opera.

"So you're Bob's brother?" he said in an effeminate voice.

"My real name's Oscar."

"How is old Bob? Still on the bottle?"

"He's okay. Studying law up in Frisco," I said, perplexed. I hadn't seen my brother since the weekend before I had enlisted in the Air Force. He didn't even smoke then. *I* had been the drunkard of the family all through school.

I turned to Norman and asked, "What'd that fag mean by that?"

Charlie laughed and they eyed one another. Norman said, "You have to understand Cheto. You know how those Italians are."

"No, I don't give a shit about his sex life, I mean about Bob. Does he drink now?"

Charlie gave a harsh, loud laugh baring his brown teeth. Norman poked him in the ribs with his elbow and I knew they had something up their sleeve from the way Norman's red, fluffy eyebrows covered his pink eyes.

"Let me put it to you this way, Oscar," he hesitated and leafed through his Oxford dictionary until he found the exact, precise meaning and etymological derivation of his statement, "do ringworms itch?"

"Do flowers bloom?" Charlie added, hitting a chord on his banjo.

"Did Cain kill Abel?" Norman spoke from the lectern.

"Do bears shit?" Charlie asked.

"Jesus, you fucking Okies drunk already?" I stopped them.

They finally told me the story of how my brother had taken to drink in the Coast Guard and had continued his daily bouts with the bottle all through junior college. "Remember when Doc Jennings threw him out of class for sipping on Thunderbird?" Norman said to Charlie.

"What do you mean? He threw *all three* of us out, stupid."

"Well, actually he caught Bob with the bottle."

They both laughed. "What pissed him off was the brand," Charlie said to me. "You'll get to know him. You signed up for his writing class, didn't you?"

"Yeh. And I'll get better grades in his class, too," I said. They had already told me of their bet to see who would get better marks in our French class, and I had become part of the bargain on the first day of the term.

"Not if you do like your brother did. Jennings is an aristocrat.

145

If you're going to bring hootch into the class, you better bring in some of those French wines *la belle* Monique was talking about today. *Comprenez-vous?*"

Doc Jennings smoked a pipe, wore tweed coats and loafers, and played his role to the hilt. He asked a young, fat farmer's daughter with finely-combed bangs and wire-rimmed glasses if she believed the world to be round. It was the first day of school at Modesto J.C. in September of 1956 in his creative writing class. And it was my first week of college after four years in the Air Force. He didn't look at her or the class. He stared out the window and ran his hand through his white hair.

"The question is quite simple, Miss Terwilliger," he pressed. "Do you believe the world, the earth to be round. Yes or no?"

She giggled. "Well, of course it's round."

There was absolute silence. The slim, slow-moving elderly gentleman kept looking out the window with his back to us. "Anyone disagree with Miss Terwilliger?"

No one responded but my heart pounded at the excitement of being in college. I couldn't recall Miss Anderson ever asking rhetorical questions.

"So you all believe the world to be round? Well, I can understand why you should think that. I don't fault *you*. I've read the same books as you. I, too, studied history. I even had a course or two in physics many years ago." He hesitated and then turned to face us. He carefully removed his black horn-rimmed glasses and motioned with his finger to the farmer's daughter. "Come here, will you please." The fat girl got up and walked to him at the window. He touched her shoulder and faced her toward the window looking out over the campus and in the direction of the foothills around the San Joaquin Valley. "Does that look *round* to you?"

We all gasped at his brilliant logic. We were astounded by his ability to force us to think, to reason and to question the findings of other men. He seldom spoke of writing in any technical sense and he never lectured in the entire year that I sat at his feet. He spoke of his experience in the film industry and of travels around the world in steam ships and box-cars, always teaching by anecdote and analogy. He grounded me in the fundamentals of the short story by forcing me to read as much of the old fag Somerset Maugham as I could possibly tolerate. After I submitted my first work to him he called me into his office for a long, fatherly chat. We sat alone and smoked in his little room filled with thousands of books. I half expected him to congratulate me or give me some prize.

146

"If I were you, I'd forget about writing," he said.

I was not yet accustomed to his dialectic and so it hit me smack in the face. "It was that bad?"

"Oh, you've got a lot to learn, Mr. Acosta. . . . But that isn't why I extend this gratuitous advice to you."

"Thanks. But I don't understand. It's my first story, I'll catch on," I muttered through bitter teeth.

"You are serious about writing?"

"Sure. That's why I signed up for your course."

"Then you and Mr. Eudy have no plans to start, how shall I say it, an *orgy* in here?"

"Hell no! I'm not my brother. I'm serious."

"Oh, don't misunderstand. Your brother was serious too. I'm making a joke."

"Yeh, I know. But it's important to me."

"What I mean to say . . . if you want to write, you should . . . when I was your age I wanted to write. We have different backgrounds, I'm sure. My parents were exorbitant. Filthy rich. And they'd raised me in that silver-spoon tradition. But that's another story. . . . Anyway, my first professor gave me the same advice I'm giving you . . . because I can tell from your story that you are serious . . . he told me if I wanted to write, I should write. I took his advice and left school. I jumped a freight train and . . . but that too is another story. . . . I eventually became a merchant seaman. And I've been writing for thirty years now."

"But I've already been around. I just got back this summer from Panama," I protested.

He stood up and appeared embarrassed. "Yes, well of course that's your decision. It's a personal matter. Forgive me if I've intruded."

He hurriedly opened the door to his office and said, "You'll learn in my class, I'm sure. But once you get down to serious writing . . . well, we'll see. But I'm certain you'll understand. Thank you for dropping by."

I didn't take his advice until the following summer. For nine months I studied French as if my life depended on it and ended up top of the class with something like a 98.7% average. I worked hard to please Doc Jennings with my short stories, but he never spoke to me again the entire year. He showed his approval by reading all my stories to the class, but he refused to let me win my bet with Eudy; he gave me a "B" and Norman an "A." The last time I heard of Eudy he was working for the Probation Department in San Jose and raising intellectual Okies with his wife, Cappie

147

who cared not one wit for Nietzsche or Lefty Frizel. Charles Johnston ended up in Eureka, playing his banjo and raising marijuana amongst the redwoods. They were both good friends and heavy drinkers, a combination hard to beat. I took Doc Jennings' advice and hit the road for Los Angeles in search of experience in June of 1957.

I took the exam for the Los Angeles Police Department and would have become a pig but for the grace of God and Al Mathews, an alcoholic I met while wrapping toys in the shipping department of a wholesale toy company on Third Street in downtown L.A. Al was a classic alcoholic. He drank every day of his life. It was his profession, his avocation, his entire career. Everything else was a mere aside. He had completely and forevermore dedicated himself to the bottle. All he ever wanted out of life was Rainier Ale and red wine with a wet towel over his forehead and a book in his hand while he lay flat on his back in a filthy, cold apartment. He too had wanted to write when he was younger, but now he settled for reading and drinking. And he read as much as he drank. There seemed to be no book in English he didn't at least know of. He quoted from them all while we stuffed orders in the warehouse. I had taken the job while waiting for the results of the examination for the Police Academy; it seemed the best thing to do since I couldn't find a ship to Africa as Doc Jennings would have preferred.

During the lunch break of my fifth day with Abe's Toys for Tots, I went with Al to his regular restaurant. We got carried away with books and ale and returned an hour late plastered to the gills. I sneaked in a quart of ale and hurried to the fifth floor of the warehouse behind the stacks of cardboard boxes filled with Mattel's finest. They fired Al that day when they caught him going up and down the freight elevator singing Irish hymns. The following day Abe called me into the office and demanded to know if I had been with Al the previous day. I took the Fifth and demanded a raise. I got no severance pay because I'd been there only a week, but I took my earnings and went in search of Al. I hit every bar on skid row and finally found him with a bunch of Mexicans at Third and Los Angeles streets. I dragged him to my car, but he passed out before I could even open the door on my side.

I was stopped at a red light in a darkened neighborhood when an unmarked, plain '54 Ford pulled alongside. A man in a black suit rolled down his window and showed me a badge.

"Police. Just pull her over," he ordered.

It was dark and I was drunk. "Fuck you!" I shouted.

He raised his left hand through the window and pointed a snub-nosed .38 at my fat face. "Motherfucking greaser, I said pull over!"

I pressed the pedal to the floorboard and my car shot out into the blackness of Los Angeles. I raced through stop signs and around corners with the Ford hot on my tail. After fifteen minutes of high-speed chase I saw several motorcycle policemen parked in the center of the road. It was a roadblock. I screeched to a halt, jumped out and ran up to the helmeted, leathered pigs.

"Officer, these men are chasing me . . ."

Wham! Right in the kisser. I protested, but they kicked the living shit out of me. I tried to fight, but the booze and the weight of four giant pigs was more than I could handle. Al slept through the entire episode. I didn't see him for over a month while I fought my first court battle. I had no money for an attorney but I refused to accept the public defender and insisted on handling my own defense. After three different judges tried to talk me out of a full-scale trial, I finally took the case to the jury and won. I told the all-woman jury I *had* been drinking but was not intoxicated. I explained the circumstances of seeking my friend Al, whose pregnant wife had asked me to bring him home before he spent all his paycheck, and how I simply drank a couple of beers to cajole him into returning to his family. And when the man in the unmarked '54 Ford told me to stop, "I thought it was a gangster . . . you see, folks, I'm from Riverbank."

During cross-examination the deputy district attorney asked me if I had taken an examination for the L.A. Police Department. I said sure and that I'd been accepted. To my great surprise he pulled out a letter from the department which I'd never received, telling me I was unacceptable to the force. I had been arrested before I went into the Air Force in the mountains of Sonora, California for a drunken brawl. I had failed to list that information in my application not because I'd forgotten the incident, but because the country judge had told me if I did enlist in the Air Force he'd seal my record and never mention it to anyone. But the D.A.'s ploy didn't work. In my closing argument I told the jury I'd served my country well in Korea and that the government was reneging on its promise. I was acquitted and went looking for Al once again.

I found him in his apartment. I had to push the door in when he refused to open it. The landlord told me he had been drinking for a month, the entire length of my incarceration at the old Lincoln Heights jail. When I forced myself in, I found him in a complete stupor. There were wine bottles all around the bed. The floor was completely littered with broken egg shells. He'd confined himself to boiled eggs, several dozen books, and from the looks of things, a gallon a day. I took him to the county hospital but they refused to admit him unless I sobered him up. He was completely incapable of walking or talking, so I carried him to the building next door. The receiving psychiatrist refused to admit him into the psychiatric ward for the same reasons. "Unless, of course he's a danger to himself or society," the squat, balding fool told me.

"A danger? For God's sake, look at him!" I shouted.

"I'm sorry, that's not enough. We have many alcoholics roaming the streets. That doesn't mean they need psychiatric help," he intoned.

"But he's going to kill himself," I pleaded.

His interest was aroused. His eyes bulged. "How? Did you see anything?"

I finally got his number. "Sure. I dragged him away from his apartment."

"But what did he do? Did he try to kill or attack someone?"

"God no. He's *suicidal*, man."

"Suicidal, you say? Did you see it? I mean, just exactly how?"

The poor old doctor was in such a state at the mention of death that I thought maybe I'd overdone it. I knew nothing about law in those days. It hit me that suicide might be as much a crime as murder. When he said, "Tell me, I must have the facts," I slowed it down. I didn't want old Al to get the gas chamber for simply getting drunk.

Remembering my horsetrader father, I said, "He has this thing about eggs."

"Eggs?" He shook his head. "Eggs?"

"Well . . . he kept saying he was a chicken."

The little man in the white smock looked into Al's face. It was purple. The skin under his green eyes just hung like a lizard's pouch.

"A chicken?" He started to write, looked up and said, "A chicken, you say? He thinks he's a chicken? . . . Or do you mean that he said he was chicken?"

"No, sir. Al's not afraid of anything. . . . He believes himself to be a chicken . . . a fowl." I looked into Al's face. He winked at me, nodded his head and to my surprise stretched his arms out from his sides, folded them up under his shoulders, and flapped his elbows against his ribs.

"Cock-a-doodle-doo!"

The doctor nearly fainted. His bushy eyebrows fluttered and

without a word he scribbled hard on his pad.

"You see? That's what I mean," I said.

"Did he do anything else?"

"Well . . . the eggs. He kept sticking boiled eggs in his mouth," I got into it.

"Oh, yes, the eggs." He wrote as fast as he could.

"When I found him . . . there were eggs all round him. He was naked. Sitting on the floor on top of a bunch of boiled eggs. You know, like he was some fucking mother hen . . ."

"Jesus!"

"And he kept on flapping his elbows and saying, 'I'm Chicken Little. I'm Chicken Little.' It was weird, doctor."

"Holy smokes . . . well, that's what I needed." He stood up and gave Al a long, hard, queer look. "Now if you're willing to sign an affidavit, I'll certainly let him in for observation. But you'll have to sign."

"Sure. I'll do anything. I think he's gone psycho. I'd hate to see him choke himself to death even if he is Chicken Little."

I never saw Al again. Betty, the therapist I'd known at Modesto was visiting that week. She made professional inquires for me from some old friends of hers who'd trained with her at Menninger's and eventually found out Al was committed to Camarillo State Hospital for the criminally insane after the shrinks interviewed him.

First they gave him a Rorschach and he told them every single one looked like a butterfly. Then his girlfriend, Dorothy—a fat, redheaded hustler who kept him supplied with booze—came up to visit. When she left, she forgot one of her pink gloves in his cell. Al jumped up to catch her before she left the building, knowing how she needed every part of the costume for her chosen profession. But while he was running around the ward asking everyone if they'd seen her, Dorothy returned to his cell, picked up her pink glove and left.

When Al got back, the second psychiatrist asked him where he'd been. State Law requires the testimony of two shrinks in order to commit one psycho to the loony bin, and this was the doctor who actually testified against him later at his five-minute trial.

Dorothy had sneaked in past the head nurse. She'd never gotten permission to visit Al. He'd only been in his cell for two days and visitors aren't permitted during the observation period. No one knew she'd ever been there. So when Al told the shrink that his girlfriend had left her pink glove in his room, the shrink just wrote him up. Al insisted she'd been there, but it was too late.

Even he bowed to their decision when he couldn't produce any evidence. "Maybe I am going mad," he told Betty when she stopped by. They kept him at Camarillo for two months before letting him go, not because they thought him sane, but because he demanded a jury trial after the judge had sentenced him for an indeterminate period.

These two brushes with the law convinced me Los Angeles was no place for me. Betty talked me into going back with her to San Francisco and convinced me that my real meat lay in writing. So I enrolled at S.F. State for a two year hitch to study math and creative writing. And I might have ended up an engineer if it hadn't been for my old nemesis Mark Harris.

After he'd read several of my short stories, he repeated Doc Jenning's advice and told me to drop out of school. This was all before the missile crisis. The beatniks in the colleges were telling brown buffalos like myself to forget about formal education. "You've got to make up your mind what you want to be," the man said to me during one of our conferences. "Is it going to be math? Or are you going to be a writer?"

I was in my senior year of college and I still hadn't signed my contract for the degree. I didn't have a formal counselor because Dettering had told me over Red Mountain that if I'd swipe the enrollment forms, he'd sign his name to them. For two years I took whatever classes we both thought best for my training. I didn't even have to stand in line for registration.

"Maybe I'll write science fiction," I told Harris.

I took his advice and dropped out of school to work on my first novel, *My Cart For My Casket*. A month later, I took him the manuscript to date and asked if he'd look it over.

"Didn't you check out of school?"

"Yeh, like you said. I'm just writing now."

"Well, I can't read your stuff."

"Why not? You've been reading it for over a year."

"Yes. But you were a student."

"You fucking baseball player you!"

I left San Francisco the next week. I was reading Hemingway at the time and decided that maybe Paris was the place for me to finish the book, but only made it as far as East St. Louis before my money ran out.

I got a job as a recreational therapist assistant at a mental hospital for the rich. Fifty bucks a day just for the bed. The second week there I met Barbara, the daughter of the President of some big Hollywood studio. I had already read about her in the paper.

152

Her parents were killed in an airplane accident, leaving her and her brother with something like $6 million. Then her uncle had committed her because she'd run off and married some truck driver.

The patients were in the gym looking at some color slides of Kenya one of the ladies from the Women's Auxiliary had taken on her safari. I was in the kitchen behind the basketball court preparing the Koolaid and cookies when all of a sudden I felt a hand under my crotch from behind. I whipped around to see this eighteen-year-old, black-haired beauty standing with her white teeth in a smile.

"Can I help you?" her deep voice said.

"If you behave yourself." I'd worked in mental hospitals a total of two years, so I knew the ropes.

After the show and cookies, the patients left. Barbara insisted she stay and help me clean up. I asked my supervisor and he told me it was my decision. "You'll have to take her back to her ward," he said. "Just be careful with her."

At that time, I didn't know who she was. I had read the paper, but I hadn't seen any pictures. I just took her for what she was: Barbara, the beautiful, soft-busted lovely who told me straight off she wanted to be a rock and roll singer. She had gravel in her white throat and sounded like Janis Joplin.

The moment we got into the elevator she said, "What would you do if I pulled off my dress?"

Because I was a professional recreational-therapist-assistant, I replied through my teeth, "Nothing. Why?"

"Never mind," the young girl said.

But she kept on. She was in the gym waiting for me every day when I arrived on my afternoon shift. By then I'd found out who she was and I tried my damnedest to keep her at arm's length. The nurses started whispering about us. My supervisor called me in to explain the rules of the hospital. "You must treat them all the same, Oscar. You can't spend any more time with one than with another."

"Look, Don, I know what you think. But what can I do? *She* comes into the gym. I don't ask for her."

She kept it up. When I told her it was going to cost me my job, she just laughed, throwing her head back and lifting her fantastic cans to my face.

Then one afternoon she wasn't there. I didn't say a word to anyone. Later that night I had to go to her ward to teach the patients how to play drawing charades, a game I'd invented. Instead of acting the title out, you drew it. It was so successful I thought of getting it copyrighted. But I never did.

A few minutes after we'd begun, the horseface nurse told me I had a telephone call. I went into her little office.

"Hi, Oscar?" It was Barbara.

"Yeh."

"Don't say anything . . . I'm in the lobby of the Hilton. My old man got me out last night after I saw you. He brought a lawyer with a court order . . . he's in the bar right now, getting some cigarettes . . . I'll meet you in front of the main office at eleven . . . Okay?"

"Okay," I whispered, my pants ripping at the seams.

I didn't want to take any chances with the hospital rules. After the game of drawing-charades, I told my supervisor I was resigning.

"But why so fast? How about a two weeks' notice?"

"No, Don. I've got to go back to San Francisco. My mother's sick. I just got a phone call tonight."

As I walked out, he said, "I guess you know that Barbara checked out last night?"

I didn't answer him. I hurried to meet my million-dollar baby.

She was driving a big fucking Cadillac. She'd changed from her hospital gown to a full-length, leopard-skin fur. She scooped me up and we drove around Forest Park until we found a quiet, dark spot behind the ice pond where we used to take the patients ice-skating.

After she had removed all my clothes and hers, she said, "Don't get that dirty stuff inside of me, okay?"

Panting like some racing horse, I muttered, "Yes, yes, okay! But hurry it up."

She was only eighteen, but she fucked like a champ. We did it right there in her car. When she drove me home, she came up to my little cold water flat on Shenandoah and we did it again, on the floor because the bed creaked. And again she said, "Whatever you do, don't squirt that stuff in me."

But I did. There is no way in the world that a man can pull his thing out of the biting jaws of a warm cunt at the moment of creation.

"You sonofabitch! We won't do it anymore, just for that."

But we did. She came to visit me every other day for a month while I worked on my book. She'd tell her truck driver husband that she was taking lessons from a voice coach. I was her rock and roll teacher. The first thing she'd say as she entered my flat, standing in high heel shoes and tons of lipstick, was, "Now we aren't going to do anything dirty. Promise me or I won't stay."

I'd promise, then grab her and start right in until the dirty stuff squirted. Immediately she'd get up, clean herself and start bitching about my sperm. "I just can't afford to have children. It'll interfere with my career."

After a month of these cheap screws she finally told me she had $25,000 in her personal savings account. "We'll buy a boat and float down the Mississippi."

"Who's gonna drive?" I asked her.

"Gene can."

"Who's Gene?"

"My old man. He can drive anything."

After we fucked we talked it over some more. I was broke. The book wasn't coming as fast as I'd thought it would. She told me we could all three live on the twenty-five G's until she was twenty-one. "Then we'll come back and I'll pick up the rest of the three million."

"But what will your husband say about me?"

"Nothing. I'll just tell him I want my teacher to come along. It's my money anyway," she pouted.

After a few days of planning, I agreed to it. I was to call her on Sunday morning. She'd pick me up and we'd drive to Chicago where the money was stored in some vault.

But when I woke up that Sunday morning, the first thing I thought, the very first thing that came to my mind . . . I've got to get back to Frisco. I've got to finish out my therapy. I've got to finish my novel. And besides, who in the hell wants to be a gigolo? Fuck, I'll finish it, send it to Luther Nichols of Doubleday and, shazam! I'll strike it big.

So I called up one of those drive-away car agencies and asked if they had any cars they wanted driven to Frisco. Three days later I was on the telephone asking Serbin if he'd take me back. I finished the book and the therapy about the same time, in the summer of '60. Luther read the book, said it was great, the story of my love affair with Alice and the fight between the Okies and the Mexicans . . . but, like I said, it was 1960 and no one had heard of Chicanos in those days. I would have to wait until after the revolution before any hotshot would pay me for writing about things that mattered.

So instead I decided to be a lawyer. Not to practice law. But just to get a job so I could write my life history without having to put up with scags who thought only they knew what literature was all about. I enrolled at San Francisco Law School, attending night classes, and worked as a copy boy at the *S.F. Examiner* during the day for the next five years until I graduated. I passed my Bar a year later, in 1966, and went to work for Tom Fike at Legal Aid.

Chapter Fourteen

My first weekend in Alpine I rolled the green Plymouth over a cliff. I had gone to Miller's pad at the edge of Roaring Fork Creek the day after I met him at the Diasy Duck and with his chick from Walla Walla and Scott, the pilot for the CIA, we sucked on hashish until our throats began to bleed brown blood. Mixed with marijuana, we rolled it in a joint; chipped into powder, we smoked it from a water pipe which Scott had brought from India; cut into pieces, we heated long knives red-hot, grilled it into smoke, and with a plastic funnel sucked the beast past our lungs.

Scott was a tall, lean, long-nosed blond with lazy blue eyes. He had run away from his father's money in Denver to see the world. He hunted tigers in India until the day he actually caught up with one. While his guides beat the bushes, he waited with his 8 mm. German Mauser—"Like Che uses in Bolivia"—for the fur coat to present itself. In a split second like a day dream when one is under self-hypnosis, the beast appeared before him. "There was no time for panic, man. I had been studying religion with old fakirs along the Ganges . . . I automatically turned my back to the monster, pulled down my pants and took a shit . . . really." After that experience he went to work for the CIA. He flew war material into the Dominican Republic and smuggled cocaine in his flight jacket. One trip he and his co-pilot got stoned before they landed in Chicago. They had unmarked, wooden crates which they were to deliver to some mustachioed, sun-glassed dictator in the Caribbean. But they had loaded up on hash and marijuana when they left the broads in New York.

"We had a number. That's all. Our only identification. No fucking badge of any kind. No papers. Just a number we had to memorize . . . the flight tower asked for it . . . but we couldn't remember it! We just sang Christmas carols over the phone and kept on smoking . . . they refused to give us landing instructions even though we told them we worked for the fucking U.S. Government," the handsome pilot said.

They landed anyway because the plane was about to crash into the city. They explained to the arresting officers that they worked for the CIA, had a shipment aboard and were out of gas. They spent a week in jail before they were mysteriously kicked out without a word. When they tried to contact their man in New York the number had been disconnected. Scott never worked for the CIA after that. He became a full-time dope smuggler and a salesman for Scientology, some new religion just getting off the ground in that summer when I learned all about dope from him and Miller.

We finished the hash and started to work on red wine. They took me into the mountains to show me the new plants. About a mile into the sky, thousands of feet of red rocks and evergreens, of aspen leaf and willow, we sat and talked heavy religion. Miller was into Zen, and Scott into tigers, so I got my clarinet from the car and called up the dead ghosts of my Aztec ancestors. We watered the little green plants they cultivated and our heads began to mellow.

They decided to climb a mountain, so I drove them back into town for their equipment. I went in, took a piss and swallowed two aspirins from the medicine cabinet, then went to the motel to pick up my stuff, for I had accepted their offer to stay.

But somewhere along the line I found myself tied up with clouds and colors and a madness of absolute terror I had never experienced . . . every long-haired freak on the street stared at me, knowing full well what I was up to. Young girls in Levis and swim suits ran at my sight. The cops were at my door, under the bed, peering in through the window of my car. Heavy fuckers with Texas Ranger outfits and guns bigger than their arms. Everyone wore weird sunglasses. Blue ones with silver rims. Red goggles with buttons. Yellow wraparounds, for the snow they said. Bicycles and dogs began to chase me. Little kids with snow caps spit on me.

I drank the hot Budweiser I kept in reserve in the trunk. But they still kept watching and waiting for my ass. They peered at me from out of cute little shops in snow outfits. Everyone owned a trinket house, a jewelry store or a restaurant. I knew they didn't want me in those places because they stared at me through their glasses and shoved signs in my face that said "No beatniks allowed!" And the law would back them up. Of that there was no doubt.

When I looked at the hair growing from out of my eyes in the rear view mirror, I knew I was done for. I actually pinched myself, felt my skin and looked at the beast again. This time his entire face was a motherfucking gorilla. Fangs and grizzly hair. It was all over for me . . . when I opened my eyes I was standing in the middle of a paved road at the curve of a mountain. *I was pissing over the side of a 15,000-foot drop.* This was the reality of my situation. It was no fantasy. I felt the warmth of my cock. And just to make sure, to be positive, to know, be certain, so that I wouldn't laugh about it later, I cupped my hand and drank some piss. And all those warnings I'd gotten from my mother finally came true. I *hadn't* been careful and I *hadn't* watched out for myself. There was no mistaking my circumstances. Somehow I had gotten to the top of the highest mountain above the valley of Alpine, which according to the sign was itself some 8,000 feet up.

I recoiled like a snake into the car . . . I opened my eyes just as the car was going over the cliff. "Well, that's that!" I summoned for my epitaph. And the front end dipped down and I heard metal and rock . . .

"Hey, Oscar! Hey, man what are you doing? Are you okay?"

It was Miller. He poked his head through a large hole in the window. The moon was in my face. It was night time. I had sure as hell driven my car over a cliff. But I was alive. Only a cut here and there. Nothing serious. I had simply died. Nothing was left of the brown buffalo. He had disappeared in the fall. His car still sits at Devil's Pass.

They took his body to Miller's pad, bathed him in oil and poured salt on his wounds. A young woman named Bobbi said she was a plastic witch from Walla Walla who had modeled high fashion in Hollywood when her man, Bobby Miller, the mountain climber, dropped out of the Merchant Marines because they wouldn't let him wear a robe and a shaved head. She now picked apples in the spring when that short kid with fat boots didn't bring home the bacon. They told the Aztec lawyer the sheriff was looking for him. Wreckless driving and failure to report an accident. A trivial matter. But he had received reports of a gorilla driving at high speeds after tourists on bicycles and little kids with dogs. He had a warrant for his arrest. Should they tell him?

"Tell him nothing!" The Aztec lawyer shouted. "Tell them you want to speak with your attorney. That's what *Miranda's* all about."

"But they know, man. He's got a fucking warrant for you. This is a small town," the mountain climber said.

"I told you to say nothing, you fool."

"I didn't. But they know. Someone must have seen you last night."

"It was that walrus you had with you," the lawyer said.

"Come on, man. This is serious. They're probably on their way."

"Where do you keep him locked up?"

"Who? For Christ sake, Oscar. Snap out of it!"

"Who? Don't play with me, kid. I'm talking about that fucking walrus we got drunk with. I know he spiked my punch."

"You mean King?"

"I don't know any royalty . . . just take me to that sonofabitch. We'll get to the bottom of this."

"God damn! Hey, Scott come in here."

Peter Fonda had changed into a Tibetan goat herder's jacket of many colors. His hair was blonder than the last time I'd seen him dropping napalm on naked villagers. He looked damned cool with blue ski goggles. "How you feeling, man?"

"Do you know where the walrus lives?" the Aztec lawyer said.

"Sure. With his mother."

"See? And you think *I'm* crazy," I snapped at the priest.

"He wants to go see King but Whitmire has a warrant for him."

"Yeh. Let's go play some volleyball," Peter said.

"Oh, man! Are you fucked up, too? Can't you understand the sheriff is looking for this freak here?"

"Be careful the way you talk to me, mister. Don't forget, I'm a lawyer. I can have you committed."

"Oh, fuck . . . Bobbi! Come here, babe."

The apple picker from Walla Walla waltzes to the fore. "How's the head?"

"Do you want to drive these freaks out to King's?"

"Is it safe to move him?"

"We can't keep him here. The sheriff is looking for him. I think they know he's here."

"Why? Did someone say something?"

"When I got the bandages at Walgreen's, Michael told me he'd talked to King."

"Michael? Silver is in town?"

"He just got in today . . . and that's another problem . . . God damn how in the fuck did I get into all this?"

"You need a lawyer, friend," I said.

"You . . . you God damn Aztec. What the fuck did you do in Ketchum?"

"I've never heard of the place," I said.

"Shit, I'll bet. From the description Mike gave . . . anyway, you shouldn't fuck with a friend's old lady. He's pretty pissed."

"Tell him not to try it," the lawyer said.

"What? Tell him what?"

"Piss tastes bad. Green. Just like it smells."

"Fuck it! I've had enough . . . Scott, is there anymore of that acid?"

"Yeh, man. I put it in the toilet. In that empty aspirin bottle."

The mountain climber with the fat boots sticks the pick from one ledge to another. He disappears behind a bank of snow. "There's nothing in here, man. It's empty." We hear a voice from out of the past.

"I had two left, man. I put them in there yesterday."

"Don't look at me," the plastic witch says.

The Zen Buddhist reappears. I am being court martialed. Peter Fonda has very blue eyes. The *indio* from the mountains of Durango despises liars. "I had a headache. I took the aspirin."

"Both of them? When?" The kid with fat boots is in shock.

"When I dropped you off . . . last year, was it?"

"Yeh, he came in to take a piss. Remember?" Scott says.

"For Christ sake! No wonder . . . hey, man you ever *tried* acid?"

"Are you addressing me?"

"Yeh. Did you really take those two caps this morning?"

"I don't wear anything on my head. I am an Aztec."

"Oh, fuck! We'd better take him out to King's. Mike told me Gerri turned him on to peyote for the first time two days ago."

161

"Is Gerri back in town?" I asked.

"Then you *do* know Gerri, you rotten prick!"

"I used to know a Gerri. She worked in a Mexican restaurant."

"No, he's talking about Michael's Gerri, from Ketchum," Bobbi said.

"*My* Gerri belongs to no one. She's part Samoan."

"Hey, man. Help me get this dude out of here. I'm afraid if the sheriff comes we'll all be in for it. Let's get him out to the ranch."

"The 'ranch' you say? Is Ruby back in town?"

"Come on, Oscar. Get up. We're going to King's place."

"The Banana Ranch? Walrus lives with Ruby now?"

"I don't know what the fuck you're talking about."

"It all becomes very clear now . . . I see it perfectly. He's pissed because I fucked Ruby. Down deep he's a repressed homosexual. That's why he wanted me to take his broad to bed. *He* wanted my cherry."

"I hope for your sake you're not talking about Gerri."

"I'm talking about Ruby. My first love. I told you Gerri was part Avocado, you idiot. I wouldn't marry a fucking avocado. What sort of a man do you take me for anyway?"

"I'm warning you, man. If you did fuck around with Gerri, you just better apologize to Mike . . . for whatever it's worth, he used to play with the Chicago Bears." The little kid with the fat boots was huffing and puffing as they lifted the brown buffalo from the bed and carried him to the car.

"Yes, take me to the Walrus Ranch. I must speak to my coach."

"Just stay away from Michael," the sly priest warned me as we lifted the Aztec into a jeep.

Peter Fonda covered his head with a pilot's cap around his ears. He had driven Kamikazes for Tojo. He had his teeth fixed after the war on his G.I. Bill. But he fooled no one. We could still see his eyes were slanted even behind the blue goggles.

"Did you ever see the USS Ommstead?"

"I'm an Air Force man myself," Tojo smiled.

"Were you ever in Okinawa?"

"Nah, I'm from Denver. Don't bother me, I can barely see the steering wheel."

"Yeh, leave him alone. He can't see with those glasses," Miller said.

"Why doesn't he take them off?" Bobbi said.

"Because then he'll be exposed, you fool," I said.

"To what? The fuck you babbling about?" the priest yelled.

"We all know who that man is. He isn't fooling *me*."

"Yeh, I know. You're a lawyer."

"And you'd do well to remember that . . . as I was saying . . . my old man drove a barge in Okinawa. Some Jap drove his plane into the poor guy. He had to dive in the ocean for hours in a mine field, looking for his barge."

"Did that really happen, Oscar?" the girl from Walla Walla asked.

"He got a medal. A purple heart for red eyes as long as he lives. You think I'd kid about a thing like that? What do you take me for?"

"So what does Scott have to do with that?"

"Oh, for God's sake! What the hell do they teach you models? This man is from Denver, isn't he? The captain of the USS Ommstead was from Pocatello. Don't you see the connection?"

"I can't see anything. I'm going blind," Scott shouted in a wailing tone as the jeep crashed into the side of a bridge . . .

Another accident? What the fuck am I doing with my fingers in my mouth? And why is Edward G. Robinson staring at me that way? Is that really little Shirley Temple coming down at me from the ceiling? And who stuck needles in Nixon's eyes? Why are his eyes so full of blood if not from hot knives? I hear strange rumblings above. The rush of monster paws on hard wood. Is that a waterfall?

I arise to find myself in a dungeon. I am in a cellar. There are huge paper posters of movie stars and political figures. Newspaper clippings on the walls. Little tidbits and nicknacks all around this dungeon. *N.Y. Times* and *Denver Post*. The poor soul must have spent his whole life in here. Look at that one. A skeleton made of newsprint with all languages, the skull has a hole in the roof with a furnace flame shooting, rushing upward. It is a dingy room. Cold and dark. Built for a crazed midget, no doubt. Where in God's name am I? And what time is it? What day? And then I hear a scratching at the door. It is thumping softly. I open it carefully. Holy Mary, it's a demon from Hell. A giant, black Doberman with fangs for whale meat. Slam! I lean against it to be sure. I hear voices somewhere. The waterfall is silenced. I hear footsteps outside my door.

"Hello? Somebody there?" I shout in desperation. The door opens and I step back against the opposite wall. I prepare myself. A bearded man with beady eyes comes in. He has a towel wrapped around his waist. He looks like a tough duck. Short and squat. A defensive guard perhaps.

"Hey, what you say there, pops? How's it going?" He has a cheerful voice. But one can never tell.

"Howdy . . ." But nothing more comes.

"Catch a little shut-eye?"

"I guess . . . say, I, uh . . ."

"Don't remember, hey? I'm Michael. We picked you freaks up down by the river last night. You were really wasted."

"Was there some kind of accident?" There is blood and mud on the same cut-down Arrow shirt I've worn for a week now.

He got a big laugh out of that one. "Oh, no. Nothing serious . . . You don't remember *anything*?"

"I just remember some guys gave me some fucking drugs . . . down by the river?"

"The *second* wreck. Don't you remember *your* accident?"

I nod slowly. I am on the verge of a panic. The water is dripping from his hairy legs onto the carpet. "To tell you the truth . . . Jesus . . . I was in Frisco . . . no, I went to . . . oh, yeh, I'm in Alpine. Right?"

"That's close enough, man. Actually you're at King's pad . . . why don't you shower up? It'll make a man out of you."

With that he left me in my dungeon. I sat at the edge of the bed and tried to come to terms with it. A negotiation of sorts. But how does a man *deal* with fantasy? When you're in a dungeon all by yourself, a giant Doberman guarding against your escape and the husband of some woman who stuck her finger in your ear is putting on his gloves at best—to whom do you turn? You got your palm read for free, you took her advice and look where it's gotten you? Salvation turned into damnation under the spell of those wicked drugs they've compelled you to take.

You *should* have known better. It has all been one long, ugly joke. And all that smoke, all those aspirins, little bits of poison, hot, blazing knives, red-hot steel as the toaster for your dreams . . . one step closer to death. Metal flying over mountain sides and the Dodge Boys still waiting for the payment. Just what the hell has it come to? Neither the captain's sermons, Miss Anderson's instructions or the shrink's analysis are of any value in this dungeon. What the hell would they know about Shirley Temple in a pilot outfit coming at you from the ceiling? What do you think they'd say if you explained, "I swallowed two aspirins and became a gorilla?" No, I didn't *look* like one, I *was* one. I didn't act like King Kong, I became the beast. Don't ask me to explain, I'm no philosopher. I *understand* mathematics but I didn't believe in physics and all I can tell you about chemistry is what I learned from Dr. Jeckel

164

at the Del Rio Theater in Riverbank. . . . but wait a minute. Just hold on. Cut! . . . The Chinese Communists. In neatly pressed Boy Scout uniforms. Not the bullshit water torture. That's old hat. I mean the brainwashing. The drugs and interminable interrogations. All very scientific. Psychiatric. White uniforms and manicured fingernails. Electricity and chemistry. Microwaves and micrograms for your nut. And if that little skinny runt could do it, why not you? If Montgomery Clift could withstand the modern techniques of Chinese Communist torture, brainwashing and alteration of the senses . . . shit, I'll show these fuckers! We'll see who can take fucking drugs. Do they realize who I am? Don't you know I can eat the God-damned hottest fucking hot sauce in the world. Without batting an eye! And, yes, without mayonnaise. Without milk. I don't even need a half a glass of water, you bunch of punks. You fucking Okies. Just come and get me. I'll show you how cool I am. We'll see who's the king of the freaks around this joint. . . . Guard! Open up! Get this dog out of my way. I want to confess. Take me to your leader!

I took a fast shower and a handful of bennies. I found an old bathing suit with a Hawaiian flower print next to Nixon's poster in the dungeon. I had burned away much of the yellow lard, so I kicked my way out of my cell in my trunks, construction boots and the CIA pilot's blue goggles. A huge stairway ten feet wide led to the kitchen above the prison area. More posters, more newspaper clippings, faded telegrams and letters pinned to wooden walls of oak and pine.

Like: "You'd better get back to that machine, mister. You can con those guys out of front bread once, but only once . . ."

Lionel Olay

"Hiding in the woods isn't going to help. Pay up. Or else."

Sonny.

Notes and messages, reminders and instructions scotch-taped to the ten-foot tall refrigerator . . . "Tortillas from Bishops,"

"Jose, the pickles are hot,"

"Case of Budweiser."

I look around. No one in. "Hello out there." Pause. Nothing but a nice, big old ice-box. I open it. Yes, sir. I like a box full of food. It makes a man feel at home. I stuff cold-cuts, whole ones, in my mouth. Food is what a man needs when he's hiding out from the Texas Rangers. Why would they leave a man in my condition down in the cell? I suck up some fast milk right from the carton. Fuck it, haven't time for that now. I see more cryptic messages above the telephone.

165

"Silvers on Road" . . . "Sheriff looking for H. Hawk" . . . "K.O.K. wants you to call M.H. at R/H Big Deal on" . . .

Some person, or beast for all I knew, had signed each warrant for my arrest with the code name of Debby. They were obviously phone messages from his agent at the Daisy Duck. Things were beginning to make sense now. I searched for further clues. The wall-sized television set practically begged me to look no further. It looked all busted up just to fool me. Then I noticed that there were magazines and newspapers all around the bottom of the floor. Stacks of print at the base of each wall. The name tags written on the wall above each stack reminded me of the post office. Of course, a *federal* agent. *New York Times, St. Louis Post Dispatch, S.F. Chronicle* . . .

And, what's this? *Ramparts, The New Republic, The Realist.*

Clearly this man was taking no chances. Why not? How would you like to be stuck up here in this prison with no one but animals to talk to? The Walrus Ranch, he said? Who knows when you'll get tired of talking to these pests, these beasts? You'll need something to read them. And why not some good old leftist literature? But where does he get that *tortillas* shit? Jesus, isn't anything sacred anymore? And the *Jose*-bit? What is he up to? This is my territory, you pale-face sonofabitch! And does the "hot" on the pickles really mean *chiles curtidos*? Is this another euphemism from the pussy-assed liberals? Do you really eat hot sauce? . . . Or are they merely being nice to me, their prisoner? Are they preparing for some giant put-on? Do they go in for that sort of thing?

I walked into the living room . . . it was the front of the ranch house. One wall was a window. You could see a green meadow with horses and cows at the base of a mountain of green, red, yellow and brown. There were large, thick leather couches around a cartwheel that served as a burnt-oak coffee table. That was normal. Nothing to get excited about.

But did you ever see dried bats with silver needles in their white guts up against the wall? A brown moosehead with blood dripping from its sockets? And how about a stuffed owl with a black rat in its beak and blue policemen's badges for eyes?

How would you feel if you walked out of a dungeon to find yourself trapped by vicious Dobermans, thought it had been but a mad dream . . . just the drugs, you know? Only to find an entire wall of this spook joint covered with guns?

Weapons of every size and description! Brand new rifles. Guns and pistols carefully oiled. All shined up, primed for action and spiffied for the kill.

How do you think you'd react if you saw billy clubs, massive snakeskin bullwhips, leathered black jacks and rusty chains all just lightly hanging from various hooks? And nothing nailed to the wall. Nothing permanent here. And an entire cabinet full of bullets. Darts and a six-foot-long bow, enameled white . . . a room living with violence. I could smell it coming.

There was a large tapestry on the wall. A life-sized, white llama. He didn't fool me one bit. The beast *looks* gentle . . . but I knew a poet in Frisco by the name of Eppigram who wore peace buttons and wrote gentle, romantic lines. *He* was a llama freak. Used to take me to the zoo to actually feed the fuckers. Until one day they caught him humping one near the elephants' cage . . .

I found a grey machine connected to another machine which was tied to a black Sony tape recorder. Naturally, the room is wired. Bugged. I followed the cord. It was plugged to a Stereomaster 342 Scotty. See those hundreds of brown buttons? Those brass nobs and microphones, the cushioned ear-plugs and the tangle of electrical wires? The man undoubtedly is a mechanic. An electrical genius.

I began rummaging through 15,000 records stacked in piles of 100s, next to six-foot-tall, black-laced speaker boxes. Dylan, Beatles, Rosalie Sorrels. I envied anyone who could work with his hands. I myself had refused to take body and fender because . . . in any event, I was *an artist*, and the man who lived in this room of death was *a mechanic*.

How else am I to explain all these gadgets. Foreign models all. A traitor to boot! I can't even pronounce those labels. What the hell is this button for? I press it. The giant tape begins to spin. No sound. Wait, what's that noise coming at me from the floor? Skinny violins. A religious tune? Did I fuck something up? What's going on here? I use my brain. I figure things out. I lift the padded ear phones to my head. Yeh, it's coming from in here. Let's see now . . .

But wait! Sit down, mister. Relax. Smoke that pipe. Which one? There's at least thirty to choose from. The snub-nosed one with the ivory bowl? How about that old corncobber? Fucking Okie! This one with the Sherlock Holmes droop is more my style. You got class, remember? Yes, fits just right into your dainty mouth. And look, there's a can of tobacco. A half-gallon of Amphora is what the label says. Regular. *Yes, sir, this old boy is all right.* I think I'll just fill this fifty-dollar pipe.

What the fuck! It's grass? Marijuana? Is there nothing in this world besides dope addicts? Don't these gringos have anything better to do? I wonder why he stuck those pins into the bats? Of course. The old-silver-stake-plunged-at-full-moon-bit. *This kid is okay.* Perhaps I've misjudged him. I leaned too heavy for a stranger. And this tobacco is downright tasty, too.

Now I think I'll just sit me down under that phony llama, smoke his pipe and put on these little old earphones—Great God in heaven, the beast is in here too! That fucking nigger has chased me all the way up here from Trader JJ's with his dirty virgin—whores turning somersaults, cartwheels and playing poker on the ceiling, "a whiter shade of pale . . ."

Chapter Fifteen

"I guess you know Sheriff Whitmire is looking for you?" We were sitting on the sun deck in front of King's house working on a case of Budweiser. He had returned to find me in another coma from an overdose of his wicked drugs and taken me out in the fresh air for treatment.

"Listen, there's nothing to worry about. I'm an attorney," I said feebly. Five or six days of drugs, booze and no sleep take the sap out of a man. After a spell you feel a constant tingling in your ankles, a buzzing of gnats in your thighs, your wrists feel like mashed potatoes and the back of your neck becomes a hornets' nest. Your hands quiver like a pound of liver on a meat rack. It doesn't matter what the weather's like, what clothes you have on. The body alternates between freezing ghosts up and down your back and hot flashes up the temples and into your ears.

I ripped the flip top off another one. I had one eye on the hillbilly and the other eye on three canine demons chasing around the volleyball court after a flock of beautifully vicious-looking black and white scavengers who'd fly right up to the railing on the sun deck.

"Don't move. Act natural." My neck got cold when I saw him looking over my shoulder with a weird gleam in his green eyes. He carefully picked up a well-oiled two-barreled shotgun and locked the shells into their chambers. I hadn't been around guns since basic training. So when he casually blasted both whams three feet from my face, I began to worry. This man could be dangerous. Why else would he carry a six inch Kaabar hunting knife on a sunny day over a case of Bud?

"Missed. Motherfucking varmints. They'll eat anything! Go after them, Darwin. Go Benji!" he shouted at the two monstrous Dobermans.

"Let me warn you right now," he glared at me. "I don't want any trouble out here. I only let you stay last night 'cause we couldn't move you."

"You'll get no trouble from me . . . as long as you don't shoot me with those fucking weapons."

"I've heard that one before," he nodded, gritting his crooked teeth.

"Not from *me* you haven't . . . I'm not like the others."

"Yeh, sure . . . you're an Aztec lawyer. I heard all about it."

"As soon as Miller gets back, I'll split."

"Oh, fuck don't start on that. I'm just giving you fair warning."

"About what? What is all this bullshit?" I demanded.

"You'll see. Things get heavy out here. Whitmire's got a warrant for your arrest. You're not in Riverbank."

"You think I'm afraid of a small town sheriff?" I laughed.

"I'm not just talking about the sheriff. Whitmire knows you're out here. He's afraid to tangle with *me* . . . but if he catches you alone . . . anyway, I was talking about Michael."

And then I remembered the squat duck with the grizzly legs. "What the hell's this about? I don't even know the man."

"Yeh, sure . . . you only know his wife."

"Gerri's his wife, right?"

"You animal. You know fucking well who she is. Don't pull that innocent shit on me."

"Ah, you fucking Okies are all the same . . . all the broad did was read my Goddamn palm."

"Then what was all that shit you were babbling about her being the queen of the Banana Ranch?"

"Banana Ranch? I must have been loaded. Ruby was the madam."

170

"Just don't pull any shit around here. All I can say is that Michael's a pretty tough nut. He said he'd wait until you sobered up. But I know he's going to deal with it."

"I'll explain it . . . don't sweat it," I said calmly.

"And one other thing . . ."

"Jesus, what now?"

"Don't fuck with the machines. If you want something, just ask for it."

"You know . . . did anyone ever tell you you were a peach of a host?"

"Most of my friends are literate."

"I can tell . . . I saw the messages on the refrigerator."

He stood up. I noticed his knees were bulges of bones like mine, except they were a pasty white with blond hair. "That reminds me . . . we need food. You like *huevos rancheros?*"

"Samoans eat anything."

"You'll need strength. Once Whitmire gets after you, you'll need it. And Michael's in pretty good shape." He gave a wicked smile with those thin lips that barely moved when he talked. He left me alone with the Dobermans. I saw him through the front window at the record player. "Mr. Tambourine Man" by the kid seemed to fit just right as I leaned back and soaked up the sun with my fourth can of Budweiser in less than an hour. Would they get me? I swallowed my last three bennies, the big white fuckers with a cross. Fifteen mgs. of amphetamine moves you just about right when you've got a hangover and the sheriff's looking for you. If you're used to them, of course.

I'd been taking them ever since I started Law School. I worked as a copy boy for the *S.F. Examiner* from seven in the morning until three in the afternoon, then took evening classes at S.F. Law (a school that graduated both Governor Brown and Charles Gary whose most famous client, Huey Newton, couldn't quite cut it as a law student the year after I passed my bar). One of the other copy boys had a whole room full of various drugs. He had moved into an apartment that had previously housed a doctor. For some reason the doctor's mail kept coming to the address and Charlie, being an outlaw like the rest of us, opened it. There were order blanks and advertisements from drug companies. Charlie got a book on drugs from the library, had business envelopes with the name Doctor G. Holt printed over the address, and every payday ordered two or three dollars' worth of samples. Within six months he had every conceivable drug on the market. The tall, blue-eyed fucker got me hooked on them. Two dollars would buy 1000 bennies,

171

and for three bucks could get all the nitroglycerine tablets a heart patient could consume in a lifetime. I took the bennies just to stay awake. For me, amphetamines were like coffee or a cold shower. I never thought of them as anything else.

By the time King and I finished the *huevos rancheros* and the tortillas we'd cut the case of Bud down to a six pack. "How about letting me smoke that pipe I was using?" I asked him.

"My favorite meerschaum? Sure, why not? . . . can I get you some fine imported tobacco, too?"

"The Amphora will do just fine."

"You fucking wetbacks are all alike!" he shouted, sighed, nodded in disgust, then went in to get a pipe for each of us along with the half-gallon can of golden, finely cut leaves.

We each smoked a pipe while "Mr. Tambourine Man" kept wailing songs for us. "I wonder what happened to Miller?" I asked.

"They probably went to the love-in."

"The deviates are having a dance?"

"A bunch of hippies were going to march to McNamara's house and give him a poster Benton made."

"McNamara?"

"The monster. The real one. He has a summer home up at Snow Mass. I hope he throws a little napalm on them."

"Don't tell me you're a Republican!"

"At least he knows football."

"You'd sell out for that?"

"I can't think of a better reason to burn those freaks."

"You don't like hippies?"

"I'm talking about the Viet Cong . . . anyway, let's get with it. We haven't got enough beer left." He jumped up. Excited. A man on the move with the white, upside down sailor cap and a policeman's badge pinned to the center. Yes sir, one case of Budweiser shot to hell. Here was a lad after my own heart. A good boozer is hard to come by nowadays when everyone wants to wear flowers and fade into little puffs of smoke.

"Are we driving into town?" I asked.

"We'll have to. You just keep your head down if you see a blue Mustang. I've got to pick up a package at the post office."

"I've got to get some clothes on," I said.

"What for? You look swell in my Hawaiian trunks. And it's a good disguise. Just bring that beer with you. It should hold us until we get there."

"How far is it? I thought we were just a few miles out."

"You can never tell on days like this. Just bring it!" We got

172

into the blue station wagon. Suddenly he darted out of the car and ran into the house. He came right back with the six-foot-long white enameled bow I'd seen earlier. "Here, you handle this," he shoved it through the window. He had three arrows with him. The buggers were silver-tipped, steel points.

"I brought this too, just in case." He showed me a little brown can that looked like it came from a surplus store.

"What the fuck is that? Old Rightguard?"

"I'm not into armpits . . . it's teargas."

"A bomb? For Whitmire? We're going to fight it out?"

"For *anyone* that gets in our way."

"Man, you really are a fucking walrus, aren't you?" Yes, sir this old boy is okay, I thought, seeing us both in action.

We began the trip into town loaded for bear. A walrus and a brown buffalo armed to the teeth. No fucking Texas Ranger would get me! I never did find out just exactly what this hunter was looking for, but I knew I didn't have forever; I only had forty dollars left and the telegram I'd sent right after I'd dropped Miller's two aspirins might not come through. Before I had gone to the Log Cabin Motel to pick up my things, I'd stopped at the Western Union and shot off a message to The Owl.

Ted Casey
C/O Trader JJ
1900 Polk Street
San Francisco
Retain services Stop Omm not at Walrus Ranch Stop Send Submarine Stop Train Bus or Plane Stop Cash Will Do Stop Woody Creek Colorado

Brown Buffalo

I figured if he had been serious about wanting to be my guru he would have to pay for it.

"Those freaks at the park put out a bulletin saying they won't allow any drinking or drugs at the love-in," King said as the blue station wagon spun around curves along the mountain-side.

"What in the world are these kids coming to? I think we ought to pay them a call."

"What do you think I brought the weapons for? Whitmire's not the only danger." He twisted his green eyes at the six-foot bow I was holding between my Hawaiian trunks. "Now reach into the glove box and get the disguise," he said.

There were two black masks like the kind the Lone Ranger uses. I removed my CIA blue goggles and fit one over my insignificant eyes.

173

"Now you don't have to worry about Whitmire," he said through the holes of his own mask, leopard-slit eyes blazing.

"Or Michael," I laughed. I started to close the glove box when I spotted a blue, right-angle, steel ruler. "What's this for?"

"They come in handy at times," he said.

"You're right. Never can tell when you'll need to measure things out."

We never did get to the post office. When we stopped at Bishop's Grocery Store for beer we ended up buying a plastic bucket full of fifty-cent bottles of Old Fitzgerald, the ones tourists buy for their hotels.

The Lone Ranger said, "Wait out here. The owner's pissed at me 'cause I haven't paid the bill."

"What's that got to do with me?"

"You wouldn't want to be seen here with that outfit."

"I've got nothing to hide. You think you look any better?"

"Yeh, but I don't have obscenities over my back," he said mysteriously.

By the time we got to the park the vibrations had taken hold. Hawaiian trunks and Lone Ranger masks fit right in with the thousands of long-haired freaks running around the little flat green park, a rock band blazing Airplane tunes under the canopy of the roundhouse next to a cluster of aspen. When they womped on "The Masked Marauder" as I carried the plastic bucket full of tiny bottles into the crowd I knew we were in for it. Blond teenyboppers with tight bellbottoms danced with young longhaired chicks hugged by leather mini-skirts and Tony Lama boots. Blue-eyed boys with tanned muscles and frizzy curls laced their heads with the headbands of many colors. Arms, legs and tits flew all around me as we looked for Michael, Miller and Scott.

"Excuse me, sir," a tall hippie all in brown leather stopped me.

"Yes?"

"We can't have any drinking here."

Before I could come up with something, King stepped in.

"Hey, Chuck Mason, what's going on here? Is this man causing you any trouble?" he said to the kid.

"Oh, no. I just wondered if that's liquor he's got in those bottles."

"I'm over twenty-one," I tried.

"The permit we got specified no booze, man."

"They were that specific, hey?" King said.

"These pigs, man. You know."

"I certainly do, son. But this man's a lawyer. Don't let his disguise fool you."

Chuck Mason tried to laugh. His eyes were sweating. He kept looking around for assistance, but the music was too loud and everyone was too caught up with "The Masked Marauder."

"We're trying to do . . . our thing, man. The big pig refused to meet with us. We had to give Benton's poster to his Goddamn son!"

"So it looks like the Viet Cong are still in for it, hey?" the hillbilly taunted.

"You mean you didn't negotiate a fucking peace treaty with McNamara?" I shouted.

"Well, you know, man . . . at least he knows where we stand," the kid said.

"That's your problem, buddy," the hillbilly said.

"What's that, sir?"

"Don't let them know where you stand . . . look at my lawyer. Now would you believe he's an officer of the court? Just look at him."

The kid in the brown leather gave me the shakedown. King took him by the elbow and guided him to my rear. "Now see that?"

"Hey, man, we don't want any trouble here . . . we're just trying to do our thing."

I spun around and demanded, "What the fuck you guys talking about?"

"Now don't get excited, counsel. I was just showing him your Mongolian spot. This boy's a liberal. He understands. Right?"

The kid's eyes began to fade out. He pulled at the frizzy top.

"Just how long *is* your hair, buddy?" I asked him.

"Ah, come on man. We're trying to have a *love*-in here."

I reached for my steel ruler. "You're not ashamed of it, are you?"

"Hey, man!" The kid was getting desperate. He kept turning his head.

"I can help you. I can tell you *exactly* how long it is." I showed him the ruler. He smiled, embarrassed, his eyes fell.

"Don't worry about this man," King said to the kid. "I tell you, he's a lawyer. He can keep a secret."

"Fuck it! I thought you were serious about McNamara. Here, have a drink and leave me alone. I've got business." I shoved a fifty-cent bottle of Old Fitzgerald into his hand and walked rapidly away.

175

Miller and Michael were sitting on a bench trying to cover up a joint they were sharing. The rock band boomed fat waves of "Sgt. Pepper." The crowd soared and wailed Watusi and carnival madness. I gave them each a bottle of the forbidden drink.

"What happened to Scott?" I asked.

"He split," Miller answered.

"Will he be back?"

"Not for a while. Here he left this for you." The short kid with fat boots handed me a letter.

Brown Buffalo,

Take the powder inside the envelope. When you wake up, you will have perfect knowledge. I have an order for delivery of supplies to Guatemalan rebels. I will need an interpreter and co-pilot. If you want to fly, meet me at Hotel Raza in Juarez. Clear heads last longer.

Tojo

"What's that?" King asked.

"The CIA agent left some drugs for us," I said.

"Well, listen, man, before you do, let's get something straight," the King said. I felt my stomach go empty. Christ, here it comes, I thought.

"I heard some strange talk about you, man," he said.

"We've all heard weird things, Oscar," Miller said.

"Jesus, what did I do?" I asked.

"I've had him checked out," the King said. "O'Hara said he is registered."

"What the fuck you guys talking about?"

"That doesn't mean anything to me. Fucking O'Hara's gone," Michael roared.

"Well, let's put it to him straight," Miller, my generous host, said.

"All we want to know, man . . . Are you a *narc*?"

I smiled and forgot them momentarily as I listened to "Sgt. Pepper."

"O'Hara said he was working for Legal Aid . . . I called him this morning," the King said.

"You guys think I'm a *narc*?"

"Well, we don't know, man. That's why we're asking."

"And if I was . . . you think I'd blow my cover?"

"Shit, man. Just tell us. Everyone's asking," Miller asked.

"Look at his spot," King said. He turned me around. "Do you think a *narc* would have a Mongolian spot like that?"

They all three laughed. "Racist pigs!" I blurted.

I spotted two nuns in white costumes talking to five little kids. I ran over to them. "Afternoon, sister. Want to dance?" I said through my Lone Ranger mask. They all giggled and blushed. "No, thank you," one with a hooked nose said.

"How about some refreshments?" I pushed the bucket to them.

"Oh, what is it?" the other one asked with fluttering brown eyes.

"Holy water. I've had it blessed."

She started to reach for it, and then recognized it. "Uh, thank you."

"I'm just trying to share what I've got."

They looked at me as if I were some freak. The five kids held their breath, their eyes bulged. "Thank you, son. We're not thirsty," the one with the hawk-face said.

I had walked about ten yards on my way to a group of girls standing alone when out of nowhere, someone struck me in the back with a fist and I fell forward on my face, the bucket of little bottles splattering before me.

"You beast, you filthy pig!"

I put my hands up to keep the flaying hands and red fingernails from getting to me. Others were coming around. They stood and gaped while some blonde whore in a red sweater swung at me.

"Hey, stop it! You idiot, knock it off!" I shouted at the girl with the huge, red knockers. But she kept it up until King pulled her off. She screamed and kicked and socked her elbows into him. "Run, man. Get out of here!" He shouted at me. I could see the crowd beginning to get nasty. They edged toward King and forgot where they were at. I jumped up and ran toward his car.

"The Hemmroids are coming, the Hemmroids are coming," I yelled, holding on to my black mask, waving the steel ruler in the air over my head.

King jumped into the station wagon breathing heavily. He'd taken off his mask. He struggled to fit the key. "Motherfucker, that did it."

"What was that about?"

"No time for that now. Take off your disguise."

"Why?"

He ripped it from my face, and spun out into the road. "They'll be coming for you, you idiot!"

I looked back but only saw people dancing with their arms in the air and hair all around. "Relax, man. I didn't do anything."

"What the hell did you bother the nuns for?"

"I just asked them if they wanted some holy water. What's wrong with that?"

"Nothing . . . but some people might take offense to what you've got painted on your back."

"My Mongolian spot?"

"Yeh, it says *Fuck The Pope* . . . in purple."

"Christ, is that what all that noise was about? I thought it was something serious."

"Oh, it's serious all right . . . that fat broad you just kicked is the sheriff's daughter."

"I didn't touch her," I protested.

"We don't have time for that now . . . open that envelope Scott left you. We're going to need some good mescalin now."

We sucked on Scott's powder until our faces turned blue, then sped over with our weapons to the Daisy Duck and demanded free drinks from Phil.

"So what's this, Tonto and the Lone Ranger?" He asked. We'd decided to put the masks back on until dark in case Whitmire came looking for us.

"Don't mess with us, boy!" I warned him. The lights were fading fast for me. The oil paintings of zoftig nudes in the bar were staring right at me.

"Just get us whiskey . . . and put it on my tab." King demanded.

Perhaps if Phil had moved faster King wouldn't have set it off, but it had been a wild weekend and Phil wasn't quite the pussy his pudgy lips indicated. When the bomb went off there were only two others in the bar: tourist-looking types, fun hogs with burly muscles and crew cuts trying to act cosmopolitan in neatly pressed dress pants. They yelled as if they had been hit and ran out screaming "Goddamn hippies!" The tear gas spread quickly and evenly before Phil could reach us with his cue stick. King and I ran out the back, jumped over the railing of the sun deck and got into the car. We saw the red light of the sheriff's blue Mustang just as we pulled away.

"There's no hope for you now," he said as we sped down the highway out of town leading to Snow Mass.

The orange clouds were fucking the sky of blue mums. I'd long since given up trying to fight it any more. I just rolled with the thundering hoof beats of buffalos at my rear. "There's never any hope for poor Aztec lawyers," I mumbled.

"Don't get carried away with yourself. Just keep your eyes open."

"What for? It feels better closed."

"You fool, the sheriff will hang you by the balls if he catches you."

"So what? I haven't done anything."

"Jesus, that's the trouble with you wetbacks."

"I'm no Goddamn flower child."

"If he catches you, you'll wish to Christ you were. Don't you know what they do with spics around here?"

"Probably the same as they do everywhere else. But I can handle them."

He drove me to Miller's and I picked up my bags. We rushed to Glenwood Springs where they have the world's largest hot mineral springs. The Greyhound wouldn't be pulling out for Denver for an hour, so we went into an Okie beer-bar and had our last Budweiser. Hank Snow was singing "Your Cheating Heart" when King said, "What are you going to do?"

"I don't know. Go to Denver first. Then to El Paso. I haven't been there since I was five."

"You ever heard of a guy by the name of Corky Gonzales?"

"Nope. Who's he?"

"Some kind of Mexican leader. I read he got busted with a bunch of Chicanos during some demonstration in Denver."

"What are the Mexicans protesting?" I asked, not really concerned about the answer. The beer was flat now. The sting from the weekend of drugs was winding down.

"How should I know? Something about schools . . . you're the Mexican, not me."

"Well . . . all I got to protest about is my present physical condition."

King looked at me and just shook his head. "You poor sap. You're beginning to sound like a junkie."

"Junkie? I got the fucking poison from you guys. What do you mean 'junkie'?"

I could see he wasn't interested in his beer either. He nursed it like a cure for a bad hangover. "You're over-doing it, you lunkhead. You've been fucked up since you got here. You're going to end up like O'Hara."

"I could use the love and care of a fat nurse right about now."

"Shit! . . . Well, fuck it. I'm not your father. Get right into it. That's all you wetbacks are good for anyway." He seemed bored with my condition. And I couldn't blame him . . . I was on the verge of collapse myself.

I opened my beat-up suitcase and took out my wooden idol. I had him wrapped in a bright red and yellow cloth. A San Blas

179

Indian had given him to me when I left Panama. I called him Ebb Tide. He was made of hard mahogany. An eighteen-inch god without eyes, without a mouth and without a sexual organ. Perhaps the sculptor had the same hang-up about drawing the body from the waist down as I'd had in Miss Rollins' fourth grade class. Ebb Tide was my oldest possession. A string of small, yellowed wild pig's fangs hung from its neck.

"I've got something for you," I said. I uncovered him and handed him to Karl King.

He fingered it carefully. Apparently he recognized the spiritual qualities, for he inspected it without a word as if he were valuing some object of art. "Where'd you get him?"

"Friends . . . San Blas Indians off the coast of Panama. I've had him over ten years."

"You want to give him to me?"

I nodded slowly. "It's a real god. His name is Ebb Tide."

"What's he supposed to do?"

"Some old, toothless *cacique* said he'd keep the evil spirits away."

"Looks like he hasn't helped you too much."

"Maybe I've violated some order . . . I shouldn't have gone lobster fishing."

"What? Lobsters?" He looked at me with a queer look from under his cap.

"Ah, never mind. It's an old story . . . just remember, it's the only San Blas god in captivity. Like I said, he's a real god . . . maybe you can use him."

He seemed nervous about my gift. He ordered another Bud for us. The fat bartender just stared momentarily at Ebb Tide. He didn't want to get involved.

King finally said, "Well, shit!" He removed his Kaabar hunting knife from around his waist. It was about six inches of fine, German steel. The point was shaped like a shark. It was the kind of knife that stopped arguments dead cold. He handed both the holster and the knife to me.

"I don't know where you're going . . . but just in case you get lost in the woods."

The hour was approaching. I could tell he hated goodbyes as much as I did. He kept looking at his wrist watch and playing with the bottle in his nervous, pale hands.

The last thing King said to me as the huge Greyhound pulled up was, "Listen . . . I don't know if I'm responsible . . . sonofabitch, I feel it. You fucking lawyers came out here to the country . . .

it's not much different than the city. There's no magic out here
. . . anyway, fuck it. If you get completely twisted . . . Jesus, I
know I'll regret this . . . if you come to the end of the rope . . .
here's my number." He quickly stuffed a matchbook in my hand
from the Daisy Duck with his telephone number scribbled in thick,
felt pen strokes.

I merely smiled. I climbed onto the bus and crawled to the
rear. I saw him walking toward his blue Volvo station wagon. He
still wore the L.L. Bean white short pants, the knee-length, thick,
white, woolen socks and the upside-down sailor's cap with the fake
policeman's badge. As the bus roared toward the mountains the
driver said over the microphone, "Vail will be our first rest stop,
ladies and gentlemen." I closed my eyes for a long time.

Chapter Sixteen

I got off the bus in Vail, Colorado with my head still full of mescalin and checked into a hotel for ski bums. There isn't much sense in trying to explain what a "bad trip" is. You simply lose your marbles. You go crazy. There is no bottom, no top. The devil sits on your head and warns you of your commitment. You see for the first time what the bottomless pit is all about. And you hang on for dear life.

When the money ran out I took a job as a dishwasher at a Mexican restaurant. I washed enchilada plates for a buck an hour plus all I could eat. After a month of that the boss found out I was a lawyer and not really interested in the restaurant business. He was a gambler from Las Vegas, probably Mafioso, so I didn't feel any qualms when I stole him blind until he fired me for breaking too many dishes.

I stayed drunk for a couple of weeks, then took a job as an assistant to a plumber. We were laying pipe for some new condominiums they were building at a ski resort. I never could get the hang of wrenches, being the artist that I was, so when my head hurt I simply covered the holes with dirt and told him I'd finished the job.

The snows began to fall and I got fired when Bishop, the plumber, found me asleep on the job. But I didn't care. I was fed up with the pipes and the tough guys who worked the construction gigs. I was sick of the booze and the drugs were completely useless by now. I roamed the mountains, soaking up the snow, and cried at the silent, white death.

I worked as a gandy dancer at a construction site where we used railroad ties to shore up the buildings. The grease and the chemicals on the 200-pound logs ate into my hands and burned my eyes, but I stuck it out until I'd saved enough to get out away from those senseless drugs, those lifeless hippies and those tourist funhogs who clearly didn't have the answers for my ulcers or limp prick.

My last month in Vail I spent every night alone. I drank cheap wine and read Dylan Thomas and Konrad Lorenz while Bob Dylan cried his heart out behind me. I knew it was time to pack up and hit the road once more when the landlord told me I'd have to quit playing the records so loud.

I decided to go to El Paso, the place of my birth, to see if I could find the object of my quest. I still wanted to find out just who in the hell I really was.

Cold, frost-bitten rain enveloped the city of my birth when I got off the Greyhound in downtown El Paso. I carried one brown suitcase of used, worn clothing purchased at various thrift shops across the Southwest, one black Argus C-4 camera, my b-flat Conn clarinet and $150. I put all my stuff in a thirty-five-cent locker at the depot and rushed headlong into the night wearing a blue Pendleton, green cords and finely-shined brown Tony Lama boots.

With a cold wind at my back I scoured the neighborhood of my youth. It was just a stone's throw from the border. Crackling, rusty electric street cars, Mexican restaurants and bars blaring *norteno* music onto gutted, packed, crowded sidewalks teeming with brown faces, black hair and that ancient air of patience which I'd always seen in the faces of the *indio* from the mountains of Durango. I saw Mexican people with brown, wrapped packages, paper bags filled with groceries, and matted straw shopping bags of green, brown and red. They waited for streetcars with their *mandado* in hand.

Every other store leading up to the border on San Francisco Street was a used clothing store. I was sober, my head was clear

184

when I saw the old neighborhood theatre, *El Calsetin*, now trans-
formed into a store for dirty, torn shirts and pants, Mexican blouses
with broken buttons, and chewed up cowboy hats, all for fifty-cents
a pound. Was nothing sacred? Is this what it all comes down to?
Can they have forgotten how Bob and I used to take the fifteen
cents my father gave us on Sundays, *el domingo*, and go scrambling
into *El Calsetin* through the entrance under a giant screen smelling
of urine and dirty feet from the likes of brown buffalos such as
ourselves? We could get into the show and see Tom Mix and the
Iron Jaw, buy a small bag of popcorn, a half-pint of strawberry
soda and a Whale ice-cream bar all on that 1936 dime and nickel
with my father's likeness.

And right around the corner on Durango Street, in a communal
toilet for all the Mexicans in the "garden" apartments, I had had
my very first experience with a woman. Her father owned *La Pinata*,
the grocery store on the corner where we daily argued for our
free samples of Hershey's kisses, butterballs or bubble gum with
pictures of Flying Fortresses and P-38's. She was a junior member
of my team. While she and I both hid from Bob and her older
brother, Sammy, she asked if I wanted to see what was under her
panties. To be quite honest I had never seen even the underskirts
of my various cousins' *chones*, so she lifted up her little red dress
and I gently touched that fatty excitement which would hound
me for the rest of my life.

Not more than two blocks down from *El Calsetin* I stood in
front of the house where we once lived and surveyed the lawn
to see if I could find my mother's wedding band. At the age of
five I had had sickness known to both brown buffalos and sons
of kings. How else is one to explain my grabbing the new rings
my father had just purchased for my mother on their tenth anniver-
sary and running out into the street with my brother at my heels?
I had my face to the wind and heard his steps right behind me,
so I threw them backwards without looking. And they were lost
forever.

When I tired of crying I returned to the depot, picked up
my bags and jumped the streetcar for Juarez . . .

All the faces are brown, tinged with brown, lightly brown,
the feeling of brown. Old men with coarse black hair, wrinkled
weather-beaten hands, Levis and Mexican ranchero hats of tough,
slick, matted straw. Sometimes there is a red feather or a green
one from a bantam rooster sticking out from the band. Their cigarettes smell of earth and burning leaves rather than of machines.
Brown, black cowboy boots, sometimes sandals of heavy leather

straps, *huaraches* with soles from old rubber tires and sometimes barefooted boys with short-sleeved shirts and cotton pants from *El Calsetin*. These men do not speak much. They look out the windows into the cold night as we begin to cross the Rio Grande. A thick man with a khaki soldier uniform jumps on board the crowded car. He casually struts down the aisle, occasionally looking into the shopping bag held firmly by some woman. The women talk and chat and whisper, they do not pay him any attention.

Women of brown face, black, long hair and eyes for the devil himself. There are hundreds of singers from Juarez, thousands of my sisters, my cousins, my aunts and the seven Chicanas who graduated with me from Riverbank Grammar School. And they all are speaking in that language of my youth; that language which I had stopped speaking at the age of seven when the captain insisted we wouldn't learn English unless we stopped speaking Spanish; a language of soft vowels and resilient consonants, always with the fast rolling r's to threaten or to cajole; a language for moonlit nights under tropical storms, for starry nights in brown deserts and for making declarations of war on top of snow-capped mountains; a language perfect in every detail for people who are serious about life and preoccupied with death only as it refers to that last day of one's sojourn on this particular spot.

I hadn't heard the Spanish language spoken in public with such gusto since I'd left El Paso as a boy. I had personally stopped speaking Spanish in front of Americans or Okies after Mr. Wilkie, my grammar school principal, had threatened to expel me. We were playing keep-away, the guys from the West Side against the guys from Okie Town each grabbing, kicking, biting and slugging to regain possession of a worn-out football. The tall, brown-suited American man who'd just become the principal the year I carved Jane's initials on my left hand stood watch over us during our lunch break.

"Pásamela, cabron," I shouted to Johnny Gomez in my best Pocho Spanish. *"Que esperas, pendejo?"* And when he threw it, I ran across the goal line.

"Ain't no good," Floyd shouted with his red hair flying in his freckled face.

"Why not? Every time we make one you say it's no good," I said.

Wayne Ellis, whose brother spit on my cock a year later, said, "You guys are cheating. You can't use secret messages."

"Isn't that right, Mr. Wilkie?" Floyd shouted to the principal.

"Yes, that's right, boys . . . I saw that," the tall man said.

"What do you mean?" I demanded. "I can carry the ball, too. This is keep-away. Everyone can go for it."

He came right up close to me and whispered, "But you can't speak Spanish, Oscar. We don't allow it."

"What? . . . you say I can't talk in Spanish *here?*"

"That's right. This is an *American* school . . . we want you boys to learn *English.*"

"Even when we play keep-away? Even here?"

"If you want to stay in this school. Yes, you boys will have to speak only English while on the school grounds."

Perhaps if I had not been madly in love with Jane Addison I might have fought the tall man, but I didn't want to get kicked out of school, so I didn't speak in the language of my parents until that night in Juarez, some twenty-odd years later.

When the thick guard in uniform approached me I felt a tingle in my neck. I had no passport, no identification of any kind whatsoever. I had lost my wallet in Taos several months prior to my entry into Juarez. When he looked at my Pendleton shirt and Lama boots I was certain he'd interrogate me. . . . Where have you been? Just who are you anyway, *muchacho?* And just how *would* I explain to him about Mr. Wilkie if I couldn't speak Spanish? And would they provide an interpreter? *Por favor?* No, I knew it wouldn't do. I knew I'd be arrested . . . Impersonating a *mexicano?* Is there such a charge?

All my life someone or another had made such accusations. The kids from the West Side fought Bob and me because we were from the East; because we wore long boots and short pants. The Okies spit on my prick because I was a nigger faking it as a Mexican. And the Americans wanted me to forget I was ever a savage with secret codes. So why shouldn't I have gotten nervous when a huge, fat man with a mustache and a .45 hanging from his waist came up to me to see if I had any papers or dope on me? But he merely grunted to clear his throat as he passed right by without so much as a look in my direction.

The streetcar stopped at the Juarez side of the river and the guard got off.

Right away a kid in short pants jumped in through the rear door the guard had just exited. He didn't pay, he just jumped on. He was barefooted, his short pants were frayed at the edges, and his blue, short-sleeved shirt couldn't possibly have protected him from the icy wind. The kid immediately broke into a romantic melody about a man who would follow *Adelita* to the ends of the earth. I hadn't heard that old revolutionary song since I dried dishes on the earthen floor in Riverbank while my ma kept us company with the music of her youth. The kid ripped into it with the excitement usually reserved for boozers . . . but all in Spanish, from a little beggar kid from the streets of Juarez.

As soon as he finished, he walked down the aisle with his grubby hands picking up coins from the people who I'd thought had ignored him. When he came to me, my hands began to sweat. What is a memory worth? How much is a nickel? Does he pay taxes? What is it, a peso is eight cents, or twelve and a half? But do I use American labor standards or will the tourist in me come out as arrogance? Am I just one of those gringos who *spoil* these poor savages with hopes of a better tomorrow?

I gave him a quarter and jumped out at the corner into the helter-skelter of the night lit up like a huge Christmas tree. Along *Avenida Juarez* one could buy felt paintings, sandals from Torreon, and sombreros from Michoacan with leather tongs hanging in the back to hold down the bushy black hair of the meanest Mexicans in all Mexico, *los tarascans*; coconut candy, peanut butter candy, *pan dulce*, candy made from camote, silver jewelry, and shellfish from Acapulco, ancient artwork from the Indians in the mountains of Sonora, and watercolors on brown bark of yellow birds, blue leopards and white lions.

And everywhere there were people on the move. Little bands of kids in thin clothes hitting up tourists for a dime. Young girls with black hair and skinny legs hopping arm in arm from one newstand to another. Young men with slick, jet black hair and pants pegged tightly against their short legs slowly moving in behind. Old women with ancient Indian faces carved from the mountains of their very own skin, old women in triple skirts down to their ankles. Old men with sombreros, large hats with wide brims, and brown cigarettes dangling from wrinkled lips. They all walked the streets of colored lights, these vendors of tortas, tacos, tamales, helotes on a stick and whatever kind of food one wanted for a buck or a penny.

But I couldn't concentrate on those things. My head was in a quagmire, twisted with the delights of the most beautiful women I'd ever seen in my life. Millions of brown women with black hair, Graceful asses for strong children; full breasts for sucking life; eyes of black almonds encased in furry nests. Whatever Alice Joy or Jane Addison meant to me as a kid, now they were only grade school memories of a time gone by. I was thirty-three when I hit the streets of Juarez and I had never found a *woman* to love in all my travels. But that first night out on the town, I saw at least a thousand I'd have married gladly on the spot if they'd given me a tumble.

I walked further into the city, blinded with love. My heart ached to speak with any of these women. I knew they had the answer to my pain. If I could only speak whatever language I could muster, I was certain they'd give me the cure for my ailing stomach, my ulcers and the blood in the toilet.

A pimp stopped me in front of a bar blaring Grace Slick and "White Rabbit." A slight, natty mustache and the same silk suit you see on all barkers in San Francisco, Panama or Juarez.

"*Pasele aqui, caballero,*" the wiry man with the faint smile invited.

But I thought, "White Rabbit?" Gracie Slick in downtown Juarez? I'm looking for a giant Rolaid, a mysterious Pepto Bismol for my hurts. I've come to MEXICO, do you understand? From Riverbank to Panama, to Frisco, to L.A., to Alpine, to Vail and to Juarez . . . and the man wants me to try some screwed-up American hippie chick!

I walked into the topless bar on the corner of Broadway and Grant in North Beach. No, it was the Daisy Duck in Alpine. Or it could have been the strip joint on the Fourth of July Avenue in downtown Panama City. Colored lights of red, yellow, orange and blue spun around in broken frames, in cracked mirrors, syrupy waterslides and flashing signals. A psychedelic lightshow hung over tall blondes with gigantic busts, short redheads in hotpants up to their navels, long-haired brunettes with cigarette holders in manicured fingernails. With the bass drum pounding into my brain, I ordered tequila for a quarter and soon I had a woman with red hair and peach skin in a purple mini-skirt asking me, "*Me compra una copa?*"

What kind of jackshit is this? I wondered. They get American girls to fake Spanish so well they speak it better than I do.

"What'll you have?" I asked.

She giggled and her tits hit my elbows. "*Como?*"

"You can't bullshit me. I know you're from the States."

She called to a tall blonde with boobs hanging to her cup. "*Oye, que dice este indio?*"

The blonde laughed and said to me, "She does not talk English."

"*Y este, no me digas que no es Mexicano?*" The redhaired lady with peach skin taunted me. In Panama I had met some light-skinned Costa Rican missionaries and in Riverbank we knew an Oscar Sandoval who had freckles and red hair. But I always

189

imagined the Mexican as a dark-skinned person, a brown buffalo. So when she threw that same accusation in my face, questioning my blood, wondering from what Goddamn tribe I must have wandered, I wanted to give her the Samoan bit again as I had done all those years of my search for a reconciliation with my ancestry. But it would not come. I could not joke about it as I had with the *americanos*. The woman had a legitimate question. For God's sake, she knew I was *mexicano* and yet I couldn't even offer her a drink in our language! If I had tried to explain Mr. Wilkie she would have laughed. So instead I took the bull by the horns and did the best I could with grunts and groans and hands flying in the air.

Her name was Sylvia and she had four children. Her husband had been killed in a silver mine in Guanajuato. The blonde was Teresa and she had become a prostitute to earn money to go to Buenos Aires where she claimed one could live for a week on the earnings of one night. They danced to rock and roll with the same abandon as the plastic witch from Walla Walla. And they both took me into the bedrooms behind the *Cantina de la Revolucion* where I learned how to be a serious Mexican for the first time in my life. If you want an exact date, you can say that I became a true son of the *indio* from the mountains of Durango on January 9, 1968. With fiery tequila and Country Joe and the Fish, with colored lights dancing in my brain, with more beautiful, voluptuous women at my disposal than I could have imagined in a month, I felt like a man should feel when he's on the lam, on the loose in search of his fucked-up identity. We ate tacos and carnitas till they fell out my ears; we danced and drank and made love for a week until my money ran out.

I called King in Alpine. Some little kid who told me his name was Jose said King had gone to New York. Miller had had his phone disconnected and Michael had split for San Francisco. I never received an answer to my telegram from the Owl and Sal Foti told me I'd have to pay him back the 200 bucks before he'd lend me more.

When Teresa and Sylvia said they'd have to go out and hustle to raise money for our food, I drank cheaper tequila at ten cents a glass and wandered into the night with the beast in my wounded, rotting brain. I was drunk with a pounding anger when I returned to my cold-water room in the redlight district of Juarez. Two old men were playing chess over the counter where the clerk sat. I had been in my hotel only in the daytime, my nights taken up by Sylvia and Teresa. I stomped to my room and felt the cold get under my skin. I returned to the clerk and his chess partner.

"*Hace mucho frio*, it is very cold," I said.

The clerk, wearing a plastic reader's cap made of a brim and string smiled. "*Si, esta cabron.*"

I waited for some attention while he looked back at his chess. My head was reeling with tequila and cold anger. Undoubtedly the man doesn't understand my needs, I thought. "*¡Senor, tengo frio!*"

"*Pues, yo tambien*—me too," the thin clerk said.

I hiked up my green cords, stood tall in my fine boots and shot at him, "Sir, perhaps you don't understand. I am cold. There is no heat in the room. I must have a heater."

The older man playing chess with the clerk looked at me, then at the clerk. He said to his chess partner, "*¿Pues, parece mexicano, pero quien sabe?*" Sure, who knows?

Again the challenge! Just when I'd thought I'd become a Mexican in a bed of whores some pimply faced old man with a white brooch under a cracked, long nose questions my identity once again.

The clerk said to the older man, "*¡Dile que si no le gusta, que se vaya a la chingada!*"

"Well, fuck you too, you sonofabitch!" I shouted in my finest English.

In January of 1968 the main Juarez jail had no ceiling. There was an earthen floor. They had neither toilet, running water nor electricity. Dark kerosene lamps showed up cockroaches the size of the pirate's thumb running willy-nilly on urined walls. The stench of shit wasn't nearly as bad as standing in the stuff in the first place. They stripped me of my clothes and searched for knives and dope up my ass. Three times, standing in darkened rooms while the freezing wind came in from above, on three separate occasions Mexican soldiers in black mustaches gave me a skin search from head to toe. The third time around I told the man I was cold and his two buddies had already searched me. He grabbed my balls and squeezed while his partner laughed and stuck a ten-foot-long rifle into my kidneys. They pushed me into another room which was completely dark. Not even the hole in the ceiling showed the bodies of the men I could hear coughing and spitting and shuffling around.

"*¡Cabron!*" someone shouted in dungeon-tones as I started to move.

"*¡Oye, puto!*" another, garbled tequila voice screamed at me. I was trapped. I couldn't move. The door opened slightly and another man was shoved in behind me. In that split second I saw

191

the room was completely covered with men stretched out on the floor. There was only room to stand around the bodies of the ugliest pirates I have ever seen. Men with whiskers bristling with lice. Men with mustaches uncut for a century. Men without hands, without arms, with black patches over depraved faces. Prisoners of war, God damn it. The black hole of Calcutta. The dungeon. Deep in the cavern of some sewer beneath the spittled streets of Juarez.

Three hours of standing and they finally led us all into a court yard. For breakfast they gave us a cup of hot coffee. Period. They lined us up and warned that if we so much as uttered one single word we'd have to wait until the following week when the magistrate came around again. I was silent and rehearsed my speech to the judge.

It is very simple, your honor, I'd say. I am an attorney. An American citizen. From California. I don't have my Bar license with me, but as you can tell from my speech, I am an educated man. A quick phone call to the American Embassy will do. If you don't accept my word, that is. But surely you can tell from . . . well, I know I don't exactly *look* like an attorney . . . but you see, the hair styles are longer in San Francisco . . . no, of course I'm not a hippie. I'm an attorney at law, your honor. A member of the bar, just like you . . . it was just a misunderstanding . . . a breakdown in communication . . . he didn't speak English. He didn't understand that I'm accustomed to heat. I'm from sunny California . . . and would you believe that your sergeant actually tried to get me to *bribe* him? I don't want to create an international incident, your honor . . . but the man actually told me that I could square it with him without the necessity for an arrest. Can you imagine that? I, an attorney, a citizen of the United States, should I become a partner to the corruption of justice in my very own father's country?

I didn't have a chance to translate my speech into Spanish before they led me into the magistrate's courtroom, a small cubicle with a single lightbulb dangling from a black cord over a simple desk which was her bench. She had grey hair and wore a plain, black business suit. A soldier with a rifle in hand stood on either side of her . . . Jesus H. Christ, I was being courtmartialed by a woman! In Spanish, at that!

"The papers say you insulted the hotel clerk?" Her voice was calm, business-like, asking about an order for cloth or something.

"Forgive me, madam, I don't speak Spanish too well . . ." I began.

"*¿Que dice?*" she snapped at the fat soldier with the rifle.

192

"*Soy abogado* . . ." I started.

She kept thumbing through a bunch of papers. Clearly the report could not be so long. There was simply an argument, a slight shove when the man ordered me out of his hotel for cursing him.

"*Dice tambien que uso palabras malas,*" the magistrate kept on.

Is there no constitution here? I wondered. I'm charged with using *bad words*? Don't they understand that I'm an attorney! What happened to due process? Where's the Goddamned First Amendment around here?

"Madam, I'm an attorney . . ."

"*¿Si o no?*" she stopped me cold. Just yes or no. That's what it all comes down to eventually. This is my trial. Yes or no?

"I am a citizen of the United States and an attorney at law, your honor," I said in English.

"Well, counselor, in that case you should be able to answer questions . . . yes or no?" she answered in perfect English.

I hesitated. The fat soldier with the ten-foot long rifle stuck it in my ribs. "*¡Conteste la senora!*"

There was no mistaking the real meaning of that order. I entered my plea immediately. "*Si, soy culpable.*" I answered. I am guilty of all those nasty things, vile language, gringo arrogance and *americano* impatience with lazy *mexicanos*. Yes, take me away to the guillotine right now!

I might still be in the Juarez jail had it not been for my ability to seize the moment. I must have given the right smile, the exact look of shame that I had learned so well from my mother. I knew when I was beat and could face up to defeat with a certain amount of detachment. When I had been told by the guys on the West Side that Mr. Roscoe didn't allow Mexicans in the swimming pool in the *American* side of Riverbank, I didn't take their word for it. Instead I took my mother's best towel, my old man's quarter and went up to the tall redhead I'd known to be a friend of my uncle Hector's and handed her my money. But she must have forgotten my name because all she kept saying was "I'm sorry little boy, but I just can't."

"Why not? Why can't I go in?"

I accepted that defeat as gracefully as I did the bawling out the woman judge gave me. "If you're a lawyer, you should act like one. Cut your hair or leave this city. We get enough of your kind around here. You spend your money on the *putas* and then don't even have enough to pay for your fines when you're caught

193

with your pants down."

"I am truly sorry, madam."

"That'll be 1,200 pesos. 300 for each offense."

"But, madam, your honor, that would be 900, no?"

"It says here you also cursed at the arresting officers . . . next."

As I was being led out by the soldier, she looked me directly in the face and said to me, "Why don't you go home and learn to speak your father's language?"

My father's language? What does she mean? I shuffle behind the soldier, I pay my fine and the man behind the tall, black desk hands me back *dies centavos*, which is something like two cents, American. I look up at him and stare.

"And the rest?" I say meekly.

"Ah, yes. I forgot," he smiles through black teeth under a huge brooch. He nods to a young man in wrinkled khakis. He brings out my suitcase and hands it to me. They both show me their teeth.

"Gracias. . . . But where is the rest of my money?" I speak with humility for I can see the light of day through the window. We are a stone's throw from freedom. "As I understood the judge . . . the *multa* was to be 1,200 pesos, no?"

"Yes, that was my understanding of the matter. . . . But, of course we have to add the tax and, of course one has to pay for his bed and food, no?"

His smile was so broad, his eyes so deeply set into the furrow of his forehead that I knew better than to press my luck. I began to walk away when the young man said, "Say, mister . . . I could really use that knife you have in your suitcase."

"A *knife*, you say?" the fat sargeant spoke loudly.

"It's a gift from a friend. A hunting knife," I said.

"You'd better let me see it," he shook his head in sadness.

Of course, I thought. You can't have a criminal running around Juarez with a knife in his suitcase.

When it was over, the young man thanked me for the present. I took a deep breath when I stepped into the sunlight outside the fort.

I walk slowly in the late morning hours through the city of sin and colored lights. Gone are the finely shaped women with mascara and ruby lips. The bars are silent. I see no pimps. The city is grey. Dust covers all the walls of cheap paint. The streets are filthy with corn husks, corn leaves from tamales, apple cores, empty beer cans and dog shit. Juarez in the morning, when you have two cents in your pocket and been ordered out of town at

194

gun point, is as depressing a city as you can find.

With my head bent to my chest I walk to the guard on the Mexican side of the border and pay my two *centavos* for the toll. I cross over the bridge with my suitcase to the international boundary. The border patrol empties the contents of my suitcase.

A tall blond with a .357 Magnum says, "Where you born?"

"El Paso."

He investigates my feet, analyzes my turtle neck and looks me straight in the eye. "You *americano?*"

"I'm from San Francisco." My heart is pounding.

"Thought you said you was from Paso."

"I'm a lawyer. I was *born* in El Paso. I practice in Frisco."

He smiles at that one. He looks to his partner who is pulling out a bag of avocados from an old Mexican woman's straw shopping bag.

"Got your papers?" the tall bounty hunter asks.

"I lost my wallet . . . I'm a citizen, man."

"Well . . . can you prove it? What you got to show me?"

Jesus Christ, I think, what *do* I have to prove who I am? I squint my eyes tight. There's nothing in my pockets but eight *centavos*. I've got a clarinet and a camera with a few rags in my traveling bag. I nod slowly.

"Nothing. I've got nothing on me to prove who I am . . . just my word."

He carefully inspects the contents of my bag, fingering the camera and the b-flat clarinet. He finally looks up and says, "Okay, buddy. Next time I suggest you have some I.D. on you. You don't *look* like an American, you know?"

Three blocks from the border I pawn my camera and my clarinet. The greasy pimp gives me fifteen dollars. I take a green room at the Grand Hotel in downtown El Paso. I sit on the edge of the single bed and remove the cockroach-infested clothes from my lice-eaten body . . .

I stand naked before the mirror. I cry in sobs. My massive chest quivers and my broad shoulders sag. I am a brown buffalo lonely and afraid in a world I never made. I enter the womb of night and am dead to this world of confusion for thirty-three hours . . .

My eyes open to the sun splitting window panes into colored jewels. It's a new day. I jump up and stretch to feel the juice of lemon blood. I pound my chest and shriek the call of Tarzan swinging through the jungle. I didn't eat all that protein and lift those weights for nothing. I mastered Charles Atlas at the age of ten and no beach bully will ever again kick sand in my face, God damn it!

I rush down the stairs and call my brother from the pay phone in the lobby. I've got to sober up and come home, he tells me. I am clear, I say. I've checked it all out and have failed to find the answer to my search. One sonofabitch tells me I'm not a Mexican and the other one says I'm not an American. I got no roots anywhere.

"Jesus, Oscar. You're getting carried away," Bob says.

I came here to find out who I was, can't he understand? I didn't want to be a lawyer. I can barely put up with my own problems. So I've got to find out who I am so I can do what I'm supposed to.

"You know what? You're beginning to sound just like dad."

He tells me he is broke. Busted just like me. He can't finance my excursion with Scott into Guatemala. He's never even heard of a revolution down there. "And besides, even if you didn't get your ass shot off, who would you sell the story to? Who's your publisher?"

"I'm not worried about that. I just want to write. Anyway, I know this guy in Alpine. He's a writer. He'll put me on to a connection once I get a story."

"Yeh, but shit, man . . . settle down. Just . . . look, if you want to write about revolutions . . . have you ever heard of Brown Power?"

"You mean the Negroes?"

"No, the Chicanos down in East L.A. I read a little paper called *La Raza*."

"No. I've never heard of any of that. Why?"

"I read that they're going to start a riot. Some group called the Brown Berets or something are going to have a school strike . . . I don't really know anything about it. But it sounds . . . more practical. Why not go down there and write about *that* revolution, sell the story and *then* go to Guatemala?"

The bomb explodes in my head. Flashes of lightning. Stars in my eyes. I see it all before me. That is exactly what the gods have in store for me. Of course, why didn't I think of it first? I thank him, I praise him and I beg him to send me fifty bucks immediately. I will take the Greyhound to Los Angeles, call my cousin Manuel and have him put me up for a few days until I get the story from, who'd you say, the Brown Berets? God damn, why didn't I think of that?

I hang up and run outside. I buy a dozen Snicker candy bars with my last dollar. They will do until I get the money order from Bob. On my way back up to my room I pick up a couple of magazines from the lobby. I lay on my back in the little green room and read all the articles. I've got to get in shape for my new career.

In the January issue of *Look*, there is a story written by a lawyer who worked for Senator Dodd. He stole his personal files and exposed his corruption . . . a spy. An undercover agent for the good guys. The perfect front. Get a straight job. Work for the man as a cover. Hell, they'd never expose me. I am too tricky. I can make any kind of face you ask. After all, I've been a football man, a drunk, a preacher, a mathematician, a musician, a lawyer . . . and a brown buffalo.

I return to the lobby and borrow a pen and some paper from the hard-faced woman with bleached hair. Sitting alone in the green room I write letters to those men who just might be able to use a man with my experience, my expertise and my vast knowledge of the world.

I tell President Johnson he could use a Mexican in his upcoming campaign. I suggest to him that I can deliver the Chicano vote in East L.A. where some one million brown buffalos reside. I hint that I have some stuff on Nixon and his wife, Pat.

I write a note to Robert F. Kennedy and remind him of his brother's dream. I chastise him for telling the reporters he is not willing to run for the Presidency in 1968. I ask him if he recalls having shook my hand when he opened up the Viva Kennedy Club in the Mission District in the summer of 1960.

The only elected official of buffalo ancestry in California is Edward Roybal, a Congressman from Los Angeles. I give him a brief sketch of my autobiography and tell him I'm on my way to L.A. to see if I can help him get the problems of the Mexican people straightened up.

Each of them I ask for immediate cash. *Seed money.* If they're interested, they'll pay. If not . . . God's mercy on their souls.

When I have finished it's dark. The lights from the bars, the pawn shops and the theatres cast strange images on the sidewalks cluttered with Mexicans from Juarez on a shopping spree. Soldiers and sailors are looking for a score. I go right up to a drunken sailor with his sleeves rolled back baring dragons on the skin-side of the cuffs and panhandle him for some loose change. I mail the letters and buy a cup of coffee with his money.

A light rain begins to fall as I cross the civic center in front of the courthouse. People are running for shelter. The winos and the fags are the last to leave the benches beside the water fountains

197

spouting water. I walk alone on the sidewalks with the rain smacking my face. I look up, open my mouth and drink.

The plan is simple. You may think me naive, a fool and a bungler but we'll see. I will call a meeting. My cousin will invite all his friends. I'll go talk to the Brown Berets and get them to hustle up the revolutionaries. Then after the introductions and the stamping of feet, I'll explain it all to them . . .

Ladies and gentleman . . . my name is Oscar Acosta. My father is an Indian from the mountains of Durango. Although I cannot speak his language . . . you see, Spanish is the language of our conquerors. English is the language of our conquerors. . . . No one ever asked me or my brother if we wanted to be American citizens. We are all citizens by default. They stole our land and made us half-slaves. They destroyed our gods and made us bow down to a dead man who's been strung up for 2000 years. . . . Now what we need is, first to give ourselves a new name. We need a new identity. A name and a language all our own. . . . So I propose that we call ourselves . . . what's this, you don't want me to attack our religion? Well, all right . . . I propose we call ourselves the Brown Buffalo people. . . . No, it's not an Indian name, for Christ sake . . . don't you get it? The buffalo, see? Yes, the animal that everyone slaughtered. Sure, both the cowboys and the Indians are out to get him . . . and, because we do have roots in our Mexican past, our Aztec ancestry, that's where we get the *brown* from . . .

I walk in the night rain until the dawn of the new day. I have devised the plan, straightened out the philosophy and set up the organization. When I have the one million Brown Buffalos on my side I will present the demands for a new nation to both the U.S. Government and the United Nations . . . and then I'll split and write the book. I have no desire to be a politician. I don't want to lead anyone. I have no practical ego. I am not ambitious. I merely want to do what is right. Once in every century there comes a man who is chosen to speak for his people. Moses, Mao and Martin are examples. Who's to say that I am not such a man? In this day and age the man for all seasons needs many voices. Perhaps that is why the gods have sent me into Riverbank, Panama, San Francisco, Alpine and Juarez. Perhaps that is why I've been taught so many trades. Who will deny that I am unique?

For months, for years, no, all my life I sought to find out who I am. Why do you think I became a Baptist? Why did I try to force myself into the Riverbank Swimming Pool? And did I become a lawyer just to prove to the publishers I could do something worthwhile?

Any idiot that sees only the obvious is blind. For God sake, I have never seen and I have never felt inferior to any man or beast. My single mistake has been to seek an identity with any one person or nation or with any part of history. . . . What I see now, on this rainy day in January, 1968, what is clear to me after this sojourn is that I am neither a Mexican nor an American. I am neither a Catholic nor a Protestant. I am a Chicano by ancestry and a Brown Buffalo by choice. Is that so hard for you to understand? Or is it that you choose not to understand for fear that I'll get even with you? Do you fear the herds who were slaughtered, butchered and cut up to make life a bit more pleasant for you? Even though you would have survived without eating of our flesh, using our skins to keep you warm and racking our heads on your living room walls as trophies, still we mean you no harm. We are not a vengeful people. Like my old man used to say, an Indian forgives, but he never forgets . . . that, ladies and gentlemen, is all I meant to say. That unless we band together, we brown buffalos will become extinct. And I do not want to live in a world without brown buffalos.

The money from Bob arrived the next day. I sat alone in the back seat of the Greyhound bus as the tires hummed along Route 66. There was a full moon over the long stretches of brown mountains as I lay back and continued to plan for my next trip.

The red sun of dawn was just coming over the San Bernardino Mountains when the bus rolled onto the gigantic sheets of concrete, L.A.'s metal cars speeding along beside rows of palm trees.

We were in Los Angeles. The most detestable city in the world. Soon I'd be at my cousin Manuel's house in East L.A., the home of the biggest herd of brown buffalos in the entire world. We would eat tortillas and refried beans and talk of old times in Riverbank . . . and some time later I would become Zeta, the world-famous Chicano Lawyer who helped to start the last revolution—but that, as old Doc Jennings would say, is another story.

BOOK DESIGN — JON GOODCHILD

Editorial/Production: Barbara Burgower,
Dian Aziza Ooka, Michael Kinney,
Douglas Mount, Katy Wolff.
Lansman: Alan
Rinzler.